SURVIVING REMOTE WORK

By Sharon Koifman

SURVIVING
REMOTE
WORK

SHARON KOIFMAN

First edition.
ISBN: 978-1-7774029-0-7
Covers Art: Miguel A. Camacho
Book and Cover Design: BoldEditorial.design
Website: https://survivingremote.com/
This book is also available in electronic format.

Acknowledgments

To my amazing wife Stephanie and my two lovely daughters, who mean the world to me.

To my dad, who inspired me to take my first steps as a businessman, and my mother, who helped nurture my business into what it is today.

To my brother, who was there to advise me through my challenges and celebrate my victories.

And to the fun people at DistantJob, for reminding me why all of this matters.

Thank You.

TABLE OF CONTENTS

Introduction

This book is by no means all about the global pandemic currently raging around the world. Rather, it was created mainly because of the migration to remote work that has been happening across the world because of this pandemic. But while COVID-19 might be the hook that gets us moving toward widespread adoption of remote work, this book is the culmination of decades of progress, for both the remote work movement and my own journey into the world of remote work.

When I first heard the news about COVID-19, it still seemed like something that was happening far away, not something that was likely to affect my own daily life. If there was any fear among my friends and colleagues, it was the prospect of being quarantined, not any fear of actually catching the virus.

I remember that first COVID-19 discussion with my brother like it was yesterday. He travels a lot for work, so I knew he would have strong opinions on the subject. As it was with the rest of my inner circle, my brother had only one question on his mind: What would he do if he got quarantined? It's not that he was feeling invincible (although sometimes I do feel like my bro is some kind of superhero). It's that the idea of quarantine brings scary images of being stuck in some room secluded like you are in an insane asylum, without the ability to hang with your family and friends or manage your company.

One week after that discussion, things got real: The pandemic was no longer spreading in some remote country you'd never heard of. It had made it to Italy, and it hit hard. Yet for some strange reason, my wife and I decided to book a last-minute vacation to the Dominican Republic anyway. Our thought process went like this: "Let's go to a place that has not been hit by the virus yet, before things just get really bad." Well, turns out that was a bad plan.

Literally one day after we got on the plane (March 11, 2020), everything changed. We started getting messages from everywhere about Corona! Schools were closing, people were being sent home, and the biggest news was that everyone - no matter where they were and no matter how exposed the country they were coming from was (or wasn't) - would be quarantined. And this included me.

While sitting on the beach having a piña colada, I was still processing: *Is this real?* I kept reading about how supermarkets were getting cleaned out, and how everything was closing. Apparently, a package of toilet paper had the street value of a small diamond. It felt like I was sitting on a desert island secluded from a world infested by zombies, and in a few days, I would be forced to fly back and encounter these zombies head on. Suddenly the piña colada did not taste so good anymore, and the waves of the ocean sounded more like "my world is crumbling" than the usual relaxing sound of the surf.

I was thinking: *"I won't be able to go out, I'm going to be stuck at home for two weeks, I won't be able to go to events, my children will get bored and antsy, I will drive my wife crazy, and I will have to work from home."*

That's when the current line of thinking came to a halt. *"Wait a minute, I'm going to work from home!"*

While I do enjoy walking one block to my man-cave/office, working at home is what I have been doing for years. My entire world is based on being able to work from home. *"Work from home is what I do, I'm the remote guy! What am I getting so stressed about?"*

Suddenly the waves started sounding relaxing again and a sense of thankfulness started flowing in. Even the piña colada started tasting better. Man! That was a great piña colada!

While for some people being quarantined might be a life-changing experience, for me, working under quarantine is what I was built to do. Yes, there have been times where I've felt like I'm living inside a natural disaster movie. But once I accepted things, what quarantine meant was that I would continue to do exactly what I was already doing...working remotely! And my entire team at my company DistantJob is also doing just that, so there is no sending anyone home and no real change in the way we are doing things.

Saying that, I do realize that for many workers and managers, any circumstance that forces people to stay home can completely alter the way they work. For some, this is their first experience as remote employees, and it might turn out to be a complete pain in the ass. Yet, it could also be the experience you have always needed and never knew about. You get to explore a whole new way of working. Once you dip your toes in, you might never want to come out.

And this is not just for employees, it's also for management. You might feel less in control and less aware of your team (hopefully, this book will help you deal with that). But you might also be surprised to find that there will be a surge of productivity, and it's not because your team feels guilty and concerned for their jobs and therefore works harder. You might instead find that remote workers are more productive, period.

It's tough to find a silver lining in these chaotic times, but this might be it. You might be forced into this uncomfortable world of remote work and end up finding a new, deep appreciation for it.

My hope with this book is to speed up the learning curve on how to do it right, so you can truly make the best of your remote work experience.

How Does This Book Work?

While this book has been inspired by what is happening in the world today, it is not just for the current forced migration from office to home. The reality is, once you experience the "remote work" effect, even when the world comes back to normal you might still want to invest in working from home more often. You might start hiring remote people across the world, and that means completely new strategies of onboarding. If you are an employee, you might decide to continue as a remote worker forever and it will change many of your habits, hopefully in a positive way.

What I'm trying to say is that this book was made for this new world in its entirety and not just for people who are adjusting from their pre-coronavirus office life. My advice will benefit remote work at any stage, for any company. Whether you are hiring a new remote employee, starting a job, choosing a fully remote operation or a hybrid system, whether you're open to international hiring or sticking to just your region, we've got you covered.

As you can see, we divided this book into three parts: remote management, remote work, and everyone. I thought about creating two separate books, but I realized that it is way too important that the manager and employee understand each other's perspective. On top of that, the manager is also an employee, and many employees do aspire to be managers.

But of course, if you have limited time there's nothing wrong with skipping to the section that's the most relevant to you right now.

This book was put together by a combination of some research, a lot of experimenting, and real-time navigation with DistantJob. I hope this will help you to understand and get inspired by this new world you have been forced into. For those of you who made this choice on your own, I will show you how you made the best decision of your life.

Why Should You Be Listening To Me?

Hi everyone, my name is Sharon Koifman and I'm obsessed with remote management!

I came to this obsession about 18 years ago in my first operation, where I was running a web hosting and outsourcing company called Empire Host. We had two offices in India, and that gave me an amazing opportunity to learn about hiring and managing people internationally.

The experience also opened my eyes to everything that works and doesn't work with the offshoring and outsourcing world.

I later sold that business. And, like most businessmen who sell their company too early, I then opened a consulting company and took on several international marketing, sales, and recruitment gigs. All these experiences have brought me to the conclusion that the key to succeeding when working internationally is dealing with a focused, fully integrated team.

That is why I started DistantJob, a recruitment agency that uniquely specializes in finding full-time remote employees. We go all over the world to find exceptional people who work from their home or personal office.

The one unifying factor across all my businesses is that I was continuously working from my computer. At most, I have had three people working with me in the same office. My world for the last 18 years has been sitting somewhere by myself managing people from India to all over Eastern Europe and Latin America. For the last decade, none of my employees have even worked from a centralized office, and most of them have lived in completely different countries.

Getting people to work from home and understanding how to manage and motivate them has become my true passion. In the past few years, DistantJob has become a research lab for remote management. Our team continuously tests new processes and new technology, and invests in new ways to create a better culture in a distributed environment.

With this horrible pandemic going on, I want to share this incredible experience with the rest of the world. Truth be told, I have to admit that I don't have much experience doing all this with no daycare and no help (I do currently have one kid jumping on my lap and another one pulling on my ear) but hopefully by the time we're done with this book I'll have more to say about that element of remote work as well.

Why Do Some People Fear Remote Work?

When the industrial revolution started, we were exposed to new ways of living from all across the world. People moved from the farms into the factories.

This was an amazing upgrade in life. It provided a steady paycheck and a consistent way to take care of the family. It also enabled people to purchase products beyond their previous means. This stability protected families from bad luck, natural disasters, and events beyond their control.

In the beginning, simply having a secure job was *the dream,* and many would put up with poor working conditions for it. But slowly, through the decades, things changed, and workers were no longer seen as just commodities. They became people on whom you depended to get creative, create products, and take on independent actions.

Companies need to attract top candidates, and that often means they need to focus on employees' happiness and comfort. An environment that fosters happiness and comfort not only attracts better employees; it also motivates them to be more productive.

In the past several decades, human resources implementations have become so sophisticated, people would see the office as their second home... Heck, even their first home. The reality is that we actually do spend more awake time in the office than we do at home, so why not call work the second home. If you feed them, caffeinate them, take care of all their benefits, and of course provide social experience and friendships, you will be able to keep them in the office and in their seats for longer.

Don't get me wrong, the idea of trying to make your work a more pleasant place is great, and I don't want to claim that HR directors are some kind of manipulative masterminds. But these sophisticated HR strategies get our brains to associate the office with both productivity and social connection. Unless you have a deep connection and social experience outside your office, your office colleagues do become your friends.

For many of us, the golden rule of keeping a work/ life balance is leaving the office at the office. When home, we don't want to be bothered by work stuff. That's why the idea of working from home seems so counterproductive to some. For many of us, it is truly against everything we know and understand.

With remote work it can feel like there are many unknowns. As a boss, how would I know if people are working? How would I make sure that people are being productive? How will we evaluate their work? How will I check if they are coming in on time? How can we have proper meetings?

Bosses and managers have spent years defining their processes and culture, and for many of us it revolves around the office. When those processes and that culture are established and a company is doing well, there is resistance to change. We all know the cliché, "if it ain't broke, don't fix it." But, often things are broken and we try to ignore it, which doesn't work. What if remote work options *increased* productivity and *improved* communication? What if there were tools available for creating a *better* work environment for your staff?

Consider the possibilities. Don't be afraid. Be prepared. Change isn't always voluntary—sometimes, change is needed for survival. But in the right hands, change can result in great things.

TAKEAWAY:

We have been programmed for years to feel that work is done in the office. Anything else seems unnatural. But it really shouldn't feel that way.

Why People Shouldn't Fear Remote Work

If your boss or employees are concerned about working remotely, nothing does a better job of laying out the pluses and minuses of remote work than dissecting the facts. According to the U.S. Bureau of Labor Statistics[1], here's how an average workday is spent:

- Reading news websites—1 hour and 5 minutes

- Checking social media—44 minutes

- Discussing personal matters with coworkers—40 minutes

- Searching for a new job—26 minutes

- Making calls to partners or friends—18 minutes

- Making beverages—17 minutes

---

1   https://www.inc.com/melanie-curtin/in-an-8-hour-day-the-average-worker-is-productive-for-this-many-hours.html

- Texting or instant messaging—14 minutes

- Eating snacks—8 minutes

- Making food—7 minutes

For those without a calculator handy, these numbers mean the average workday includes two hours and fifty-three minutes of productive work. How do you like them apples?!

There's more. According to a survey done by Coco Cloud[2], remote workers are 77 percent more productive, 52 percent are willing to take less time off, and 23 percent are willing to work more hours in return for working from home. Working from home means no commute. Less money is spent on gas, vehicle maintenance, and unpaid time. People who work from home are not pressed to make it home at the end of the workday. They take less sick time and are willing to work more hours. Think about it. The main cure for not feeling well is to rest. When tired of sleeping, the computer will call, and work will be done.

This is not possible when working in an office with other people. For fear of infecting others, people stay home the entire day—sometimes several days—and work productivity comes to a screeching halt.

---

2   https://www.cosocloud.com/press-releases/coso-survey-shows-working-remotely-benefits-employers-and-employee

You can argue that working remotely has some of the same elements as taking a vacation (or at least less of the everyday grind of commuting that necessitates vacations), so you need less of it. Many employees do spend a bit more time working, and more important than that, they don't leave small projects in the middle because they are in a rush to get back home.

Here's another piece of relevant research: According to the MIT Sloan School of Management[3], remote employees are happier and more independent. This means you actually need to manage them less, and they will be more productive.

Did you have enough? Because I have more.

When you choose to go remote, you can suddenly go international. Then your recruitment process will get easier, because the world is just big, and you'll no longer limit yourself by geography. When people think internationally, often they think about the fact that people work in countries where the cost of living is lower; but that's not the only advantage. When you choose to expand beyond your limited region, you can find people who are a better fit for your requirements.

I know this might sound discouraging for people who work within your region, but once they think globally, an entire world of possibility opens. Western

---

3 https://sloanreview.mit.edu/article/should-your-company-embrace-coworking/

employees who are threatened by international competition within the job market can also find international opportunities that fit better and make them happier. Suddenly an American can find a better fit in a British company, which was not a real option in the past.

Last but not least, you can become a truly green company. There are very few better solutions for the environment than going remote and cutting back on the pollution that comes from many different forms of travel.

If all the people who switched to remote work during the COVID-19 crisis stay remote afterward, we could eliminate 54 million tons of greenhouse gas in the U.S. alone. That is about 10% of the total 5 billion tons of greenhouse gas produced in the U.S. per year. To top it off, offices, which are being used only 50% of the time, still waste a significant amount of energy in lighting, heating, cooling, and electricity usage. Have you ever passed an office building at night? Were the lights still on, as if people were having a huge party all night and you were not invited? It happens often, and it is a huge waste.

This leap might sound scary for many people. But going remote opens up an entire horizon to a happier, more productive world, with fewer cluttered roads and more fresh air.

TAKEAWAY:

Remote workers are happier, more motivated, take fewer sick days, are less distracted, and cause less damage to the environment. Moreover, going beyond your limited region gives you access to a much bigger pool of people who work from countries where the cost of living is much lower, creating a win-win situation for both those workers and your company.

The Politics of Remote Work

OK, let's discuss the huge pink elephant in the room. For many people, remote work promotes the idea of outsourcing and cheap labor, which immediately turns into fear of losing western jobs. Politicians and the media have suggested this for years. They say people are losing their jobs and businesses are closing because of cheap labor across the world. Yet, with the exception of black swan events such as the burst of the dot com bubble or the banking crisis of 2007-2008, unemployment rates in the United States have stayed approximately the same, if not improved, every year going back multiple decades.

This might sound quite unusual. India and the Philippines have been gaining hundreds of millions of jobs in the outsourcing service market—jobs that once belonged to Americans and other western residents—yet the unemployment rate did not budge in those countries. How's that possible?

Well, all we have to do is inspect some economic laws. When we start providing a bunch of new jobs to people that did not have jobs before, we are creating more consumers. When I first went to India in the early 2000s, I noticed tons of McDonald's and Pizza Huts and U.S. clothing brands like Nike and Reebok. My associate at the time told me these businesses did not exist in India 10 years earlier. With the economic boom, suddenly new brands and new industries found opportunities in other countries. And guess what? Almost all of them were American and European companies. In other words, when a western company employs people outside their country, they are not just creating jobs somewhere else. They are also creating consumers who will purchase the products that generate jobs in the first place.

The reason why we have a perception that unemployment is increasing is because we like to show the jobs that were lost to the cheap labor market, but we never discuss the jobs that are being created. We never follow up or alert people a few months later about where the people that lost their jobs are at the moment. What happened to the people who lost their jobs to a cheaper labor market? Based on employment rates, they found employment elsewhere, often somewhere potentially more challenging and more creative.

Don't get me wrong. I'm not saying the U.S. doesn't have some employment challenges, and we do need to define what is considered a quality job. Still, outsourcing, offshoring, or hiring international staff has very little negative effect on employment rates. The only effect that you do actually have is drastically lowering poverty rates in other countries. That's right, the effect of international hiring is as the expression goes, don't give a man a fish, teach him how to fish. You just taught someone how to fish, so you no longer need to give charity.

Here's another interesting side effect: One of the biggest industries to be outsourced to India and the Philippines was the call center industry. Because richer countries helped create a stronger economy within less wealthy countries, the salary of an American call center employee is currently just 15 percent higher than the ever increasing salary of a call center employee in India. Now jobs are coming back. Isn't that amazing? We brought entire economies out of poverty, created more consumption, and at the same time, jobs are returning to the U.S.

Two other industries that gained a reputation for losing jobs to the outsourcing industry are IT and software development. I have talked to people who had a friend of a cousin from their stepmother's side who lost their job to someone in India or Ukraine... bad news, for sure. Yet once we get down to the facts, the need for software engineers doubles every five years, and the age and experience of candidates go down every day. No one is running out of work; we are running out of engineers. This equalizes the financial playing field very quickly.

As a side note, the reason why I'm not delving too much into China, the other beast of the offshore world, is because China has political issues (or should I say dictatorship issues) that negatively affect human rights and environmental concerns. While it is pretty amazing that the western world contributed to China's climb from poverty, the economic influence that China is gaining comes with quite a few problems. But that is a discussion for another book.

The only real fear we should have from international hiring is when we start losing the ideas and creative battle. The key is having the people and companies that can think outside the box to create a new product and new brand, and cheap labor won't provide that. What will , is working with happier, more independent employees, and as we learned in the previous section, there is no better way to accomplish that goal than hiring remote workers.

So why do the politics of remote work matter so much?

There's this old book called *Secrets of the Millionaire Mind*. It was one of those self-help motivational books focused on making money. Now if you are one of those people who are interested in reading it, I might ruin it for you, because it can be summarized with one phrase: Don't be afraid to make money, and don't be afraid to be successful.

The upshot of this book is that running a business is incredibly tough. The word on the street since I first entered the business world is that one out of ten people succeed in business. I don't actually know how precise this statistic is and how many of these ten people just registered for a business—but then didn't really do much. Yet, let's say even if it's one out of four people, this mountain that you are trying to climb comes with massive falling rocks and the slipperiest ice. Because building a business is so difficult, psychologically you cannot afford to have unnecessary obstacles, be they emotional or political. If you feel that making money or being successful is wrong or evil, you are simply doomed to fail.

So why bring all this up in a book about remote work? Because remote work comes with a lot of prejudgments and fears, similar to the ones that we have seen above. When I see a new client that comes with a horrible attitude that he is only hiring because he doesn't have a choice, it's almost always a failure. I have had so many experiences where I go to a conference, hang with a CEO, and get him excited about using our service. The CEO comes back to the office pumped up like a perky cheerleader, excited about opening the world to new talents. He tells his CTO to work with our company, but the CTO doesn't have the same enthusiasm, and is actually dreading the idea.

So while I love the prospect of getting a new client, I know that it will be a very difficult process, one which will almost always fail. My goal with this book is to get you as pumped up about remote work as that CEO... or as I am! I want you to put your pom poms in the air and say, "YAYYYYY, REMOTE WORK!" If you don't come into this with an optimistic approach, you are drastically hurting your chances of succeeding. I hope this book will help you find that optimism.

TAKEAWAY(S):

- **International Job = consumers = Western products are being purchased = more jobs in Europe and North America = no one loses jobs = more jobs all around = less need for charity**

- **Understanding the politics = being proud of your work = doing a better job**

Part I - Management

I - MAKING THE BIG MOVE

By the time many of you read this book, COVID-19 may have pushed you to move part of your team or even the entire office to remote work. Or hey, maybe the pandemic has nothing to do with the decision to go remote; I mean there are murder hornets on the loose who could also keep you at home! Considering how crazy 2020 has been, maybe we'll see an invasion of aliens who want to use our offices to hang out. Whatever your reason to migrate, there are some fundamentals that you need to think about if you want to make the shift to a remote culture work for your company.

Words Matter (understanding the language of remote work and where it comes from)

Alright, we are ready, it's time to get started. We want to be awesome remote managers. What is the first thing we should think about? Surprisingly, it's the language that we use in relation to the world of remote work. In this world, words most definitely matter.

To understand the importance of language when it comes to remote work, some historical perspective is in order.

I will skip the entire manufacturing industry, which built the Chinese economy and that of a few other Eastern countries because our focus is mostly about the service industry. This brings us to India. We start our journey there about 30 years ago, when the multi-billion-dollar outsourcing industry was born. Now for any sticklers out there, I don't know if the first outsourced company was based in India, but India was definitely the country that popularized outsourcing services in the early 90s. The reason for the growth of the outsourcing industry in India relates to the country's strong emphasis on education, especially in IT. It's also due to the country's large community of English speakers, making globalization a reality. Oh yeah, let's not forget the most important aspect: a lower cost of living, and thus lower wages than companies would have to pay workers in, say, New York City or London.

Just to be clear, the real definition of outsourcing is not working with foreign countries. Rather, it's offloading work to another company when you don't have the competencies in-house. The real name of what most of us call outsourcing these days is offshore outsourcing. Yet, to be fair, the term outsourcing has been widely accepted.

With the mass growth of outsourcing solutions in India and other Asian countries, cost became the main reason for companies to outsource. But the emphasis on cost caused people to miss another much bigger advantage to hiring internationally, which is access to talent. Simply when you choose to go beyond your region, you have access to a much bigger pool of talent, which means being able to hire a better fit, much faster. Unfortunately, the reality of the early days of outsourcing is that employers who wanted to benefit from this massive pool of talent had to go through an outsourcing company...unless they could afford to open their own overseas office. That means they would pick a provider, write very detailed job descriptions and get a quote to approve. The only step left after that was to pray that the product came back somewhat close to what you'd described.

This is not an exaggeration, especially in the early stages. Working with an outsourcing company was somewhat of a gamble. It was hard to know which one of these foreign companies really knew what they were doing. Even if you landed on a competent company, that firm's goal was to move along as many projects as possible, which did not leave a lot of room for that extra loving touch.

If you ran a real estate company, trying to design a website, offshore outsourcing was a reasonable option, because you didn't have these competencies in house. But the unusual aspect of that time was that many companies, such as software development and marketing agencies, outsourced some of their core skills, just because of the cost advantage.

In return, they often got unfocused managers who took on multiple projects, and workers they had no control over. Forget about people fully investing in the process of your company and integrating into your culture.

The outsourcing industry eventually understood the value of fully-focused, integrated individuals and started providing full-time staff who worked explicitly for one company. It was called dedicated staffing, or, later on, out-staffing. This was no doubt a great evolution, but it did come with a few challenges. First, the staff member still wasn't really integrated into your company culture, considering he was working in an office full of bosses and colleagues that he hangs out with, all of whom work for different companies. Outsourcing also has the same limitation of a local recruitment agency, in that it usually limits hiring to a specific region surrounding the physical office. Hey, just because it's international does not automatically make it remote.

Suddenly there was access to marketplaces like Elance and Freelancer.com, business models that provided access to many outsourcing companies across the world, and even more individuals who decided to work on their own, the freelancers. Now, finally, you had the benefit of having the entire world in your hand, reaching legions of service providers without being limited to a region of a specific office. Still, freelancers also came with some disadvantages that were quite similar to those found among outsourcing companies.

They had no choice but to always be in a biz dev mode, always thinking about the next project, sometimes taking on more than one project at a time. Some of these freelancers were really fortunate to get fully integrated into the company and become real remote employees, but many made a choice of staying freelancers because they loved the lifestyle and flexibility. The fact that these one-person businesses made a choice not to become fully-fledged outsourcing companies was often because their goal was more flexibility to work from wherever and whenever they wanted. In other words, these individuals were not highly focused on integrating into your company because they enjoyed the individualism of the work.

Another small change that has happened in the last decade is that many companies and individuals stopped calling themselves freelancers and outsourcers. Instead they evolved into contractors and consulting firms to remove the stigma that comes with the outsourcing industry. So, while all the terms might sound different, they do pretty much accomplish the same thing.

Of course, in the modern era, it is possible to simply hire people across the world and let them work remotely. These days, the quality of the Internet and accessible technology lets anyone work professionally from home and truly integrate as part of the company, even if they live on the other side of the world.

Now, why am I telling you all this? Firstly, so you understand what it truly means to be a remote employee. It is someone who wants a full-time permanent job and wants to be part of something bigger than themselves. Too many times, clients come to me and ask, "Hey, could you find me a person to work for six months or part-time?' I always need to clarify "that you are not looking for an employee, you are looking for a freelancer, and that comes with a lot less investment on behalf of the worker."

Remote employees are not looking to work from the beach or try to grow their own operation. They are with you for the long run and that's why you need to make sure that you treat the person like a real employee. That process all starts with words.

I sometimes find myself fighting with some of my clients to stop calling the individuals that DistantJob finds for them freelancers or outsourced staff. That also includes consultants, or contractors. These terms have a finite meaning to them and they sound like a person who declares her own hours and will quickly want to move on.

A remote employee loves the benefit of working from home or a close office, but for lack of better words, he is there to sit on his ass during his working hours and produce. Most importantly, it is an individual who is highly motivated to learn your methods and is interested in contributing to the team.

Now, I have to clarify one thing: There is nothing wrong with people who get paid like contractors if that is the most financially beneficial way to compensate them. It is something very different when someone actually functions like a contractor and freelancer irrelevant to the financial arrangement. The feeling of being part of a team matters so much no matter how you get paid, and it all starts with the language you choose to use.

The terms outsourced employee, freelancer, contractor, and consultant all fit into one category, which I call noncommittal workers. Calling someone by those terms will immediately distance your worker. It will make her feel like an extra, a faceless number, someone who is used for a specific service, even if it is a long-term project.

The terms you should be using are employee, staff member, teammate, colleague, manager, or partner. These terms change the way a person sees the company, and strangely enough, changes the way a manager or boss sees that worker. Employees are people you invest in, you integrate, and you make sure to feel like part of a team. They, in return, feel the job is an investment in themselves. They feel part of the team and want to make it a better working environment.

TAKEAWAY:

No matter where they are and how they get paid, if you label your worker with noncommittal terms such as "freelancer," "outsourced employee," or "consultant," you will hurt your chances of having fully invested employees. Stick to terms such as "workers," "staff," "managers," and "colleagues."

Bringing Employees Closer

Of course, words are just the beginning. You can't just call someone an employee and not treat them as such. So, the big question is, how do you make a person who works from a distance feel like he is one of your local yokels?

Well, surprisingly, it's easier than you might think. Invest in a quality camera, reliable Internet service, and good headphones. Make sure your employees have the same equipment on their side, and that they know how to use the equipment. Then, enjoy a real conversation.

At first, you might tell yourself it's not the same. But why not? Think about it this way. When you work in an office environment, how do you manage your people?

If it's anything like many of my friends who hold management positions, you go to the cubicle or the office of the person next to you, you check on them, you see how they are progressing, you fix their problem, you motivate them, give them some words of inspiration, and go to your next individual.

So, the question is, what stops you from doing this with a webcam? Walking to another cubicle could take 30 seconds, walking to another floor could take even five minutes. Turning on a camera takes 10 seconds and maybe another 10 seconds to find out if the person is there. That's far better than the office experience, where walking to the specific person you want to talk to wastes time and distracts others.

There are now many conferencing tools and work-sharing tools that make it far easier to see what your worker has accomplished rather than standing behind him awkwardly staring at his bald spot while trying to correct his errors.

I know it might feel strange, but almost nothing changes when you are in the same place; the only thing you can do is infringe on someone's personal space. So turning on your camera and starting the process, it's that easy. It might seem more complicated and awkward, but that's just inside your head.

Once you and your staff get used to communicating using technology, you'll wonder why you made such a big deal about avoiding it in the first place. The key is to get your people on cam as much as possible. Text chat might work for quick messages, but you should avoid long discussions on text.

I need to add a few more words about webcams. In one way it is not necessary to use a webcam all the time. But when there are real meetings that involve brainstorming, discussing serious and complicated issues, interviewing, and even simply socializing, the webcam is an absolute must.

Bosses in a physical office use their phones all the time, so the idea of having a few more chats on the phone now that you are remote may not seem like a big deal...but it is.

In the office, you have plenty of facetime and because of the disconnect of remote, you actually need even more. Seeing someone's face and even hand motions has a very important psychological effect. It allows you to connect better with people. You get to see lots of nonverbal communication that lets you evaluate people's effort, motivation, and mental health. This does not mean that you have to interrupt people all the time to get on the video with you, nor does it mean that you can't, once in a while when you are on the road or even walking, use non-visual communication. Still, face-time is essential to maintain a good relationship with remote workers.

Of course, treating a remote worker like a full-fledged employee also means giving them the same benefits as in-house staff. Although they are getting the best benefit ever—to work from home—consider offering more. Nothing says, "You're not a contractor or outsourced employee," like offering the same paid days off as your local employees. Even if the person works on a part-time contract, by allowing for sick days, vacation, holidays, and two weeks' severance pay, your remote staff will feel like part of the crew. They will want to invest in your company. With a mobile worker health insurance provider like Safetywing, you can even provide health insurance. I know it's not necessarily easy to give a remote worker all the benefits on an international level, but do your best to level the playing field.

TAKEAWAY:

Make sure that you and your employees have good headsets and cameras, so that you can communicate as effectively as you would in the office. The more you communicate on webcam, the more you will see that not much has changed, and that your remote employee can feel like any other employee. Try as much as possible to replicate the benefits that would usually come with the office, such as health care, holidays, and vacations. You have to try and level the playing field as much as possible.

Reevaluate Your Management Skills

Remote management forces you to do all the things you should have done in the first place.

Now, this might be a bit of a tough pill to swallow, and I hope it will not turn off anyone from reading this. The reason why remote management might be awkward for some managers is that they might not be so good at it in the first place. Of course, I'm not talking about you, Captain Awesome, you are an amazing manager...that's why you are reading this book! I'm talking about the other guy. Yeah, the other guy, of course. But, on a serious note, managers truly learn about themselves when they start working with remote people.

The reality is that the strategies that you use with your remote team shouldn't be very different. Checking on staff, making sure they feel part of the team, making sure they are included, making sure they are motivated, making sure they are productive, making sure they deliver on time, making sure they are in the right headspace, and making sure they understand the company's culture and processes...these are all things a manager should be doing with local employees already.

The only difference is that with local employees, a manager can get away with doing a bad job for much longer. There is a certain cross check in an office environment, where if you start smelling like you haven't showered in six weeks and dress like the corner squeegee kid, your colleagues will notice that something is wrong (that's assuming you are not into the squeegee look). It's much easier to notice burnouts and depression or when team members are simply not into their work when you are surrounded by people who are participating in the same activity day in and day out.

Just being in an office space, staff can feel part of a team where everyone does seem to feel more included. With enough time a team can even define the company's culture. Still, if the manager takes her hands off the steering wheel, things will eventually fall apart, and it will be much harder to fix when that happens.

When things don't work well in a remote environment, they fail much faster, and it's much easier to pinpoint the damage, which unfortunately is often related to the manager. In an office environment, when the damage is caused, it is usually caused at a much slower pace, and when there are smaller negative transitions it is much harder to find the bottleneck. It's like someone who has his bones broken; you put a cast on, and within a few months, they're as good as new. But when your joints have been slowly damaged through years of bad habits, it is much harder to pinpoint and repair the problem. (Ask my physio, I'm talking from experience!)

The fact that many employees have been forced to work remotely puts managers to the test to see if they have been following proper processes. For some of you managers, this might be scary. because you might find out something about yourself that you might not like. But for many, this is an exciting opportunity to learn and understand what's prevented you from reaching the next level.

My motto is this: A great manager is a great remote manager. With the right technology and a few small adjustments, the skills required to do the job should be the same.

> ## TAKEAWAY:
>
> Going remote might be a wakeup call for some managers. See this as an opportunity to get better.

An Opportunity To Improve As A Leader

Replicating the experience of an office in a remote environment might be easier than you think; just keep in mind that not everything in your office is so great. In many companies, meetings are an incredible waste of time. The office can be an incredibly distracting place, and our processes for evaluating productivity are often confused with the number of hours we spend typing on a keyboard.

The truth is that many offices do not manage distractions well and do not evaluate the effectiveness of meetings. Some offices don't have established management methodologies for productivity. Others do follow management methodologies like a cult, yet don't take the time to properly evaluate if those methodologies actually work. In other words, not everything in the office needs to be replicated for a remote working environment to be successful.

Just like moving a house, when there is such a transition of moving people from their office to their home, it is the perfect time to create a management garage sale for all the processes that did not work so well. It's also a great time to acquire a new management strategy that could fit well in your living room. This is the time to improve on the business strategy that you should have implemented a while ago but couldn't because of bureaucracy and bottlenecks. This could also be the opportunity to eliminate the bureaucracies and bottlenecks that have prevented you from making quick changes in the first place.

At DistantJob, continuously experimenting with different methodologies and processes gave me the opportunity to create a company with happier, more independent individuals. It took a while to find the right methodologies because not only was it hard to find the right process for the company, each department needed something a bit different.

It wouldn't be possible to implement if I didn't have an environment well suited to making quick changes. Unfortunately, we do not always have the luxury of removing bureaucracies, whether we like them or not. Most big companies have a much bigger footprint that can make it hard to avoid red tape. Still, if you are implementing a big migration, whether your company is big or small, this is your opportunity to learn and implement something interesting. Here's another cool thing about all this: Because there's almost always chaos during a big migration or any type of big company change, no one can blame you if you make some mistakes along the way.

Remote work forces you to get out of your comfort zone, and that might be the best thing to ever happen to you and your company. If you don't know where to start, here are some questions you can ask yourself. These will help you define what types of changes you can potentially implement for yourself and for your company:

1. Am I managing my employees' distractions?

2. Am I paying attention to the bottlenecks in the company?

3. Am *I* a bottleneck in the company? (This might lead to a rude awakening!)

4. Am I giving my employees opportunities to evolve and shine?

5. Am I communicating well with my employees?

6. Does my team communicate well with me?

7. Do my employees feel confident asking me anything?

8. Do I have my team's trust, so that they can communicate with me about anything, without worrying about consequences? (Put another way, do your employees feel confident telling you that you suck?)

9. Do I create a safe environment for constructive conflict?

10. Do my employees work well with each other?

11. Am I aware of my employees' mental state?

12. Am I getting new ideas or creating action plans from meetings?

If you are answering no or I don't know to many of these questions, read on. This book will cover all of these points, and more.

It's The Work, Stupid!

The Goal, written by Eliyahu Goldratt, is one of the great management books studied in most MBA programs. It is an unusually fun book, because it was written as a novel instead of just a dry old boring business book. Still, the lessons that the book teaches are fundamental for any business. The story follows Alex Rogo, a manager who can't get his factory to produce on time. He has evaluated his management by his ability to keep people busy, believing that's a sign of efficiency. Eventually, he finds a mentor named Jonah, who teaches him that the reason his factory can't produce on time is that he focuses on efficiencies and not throughput, another word for how much product goes through a production line. Jonah teaches Alex to define and work on the bottlenecks within processes, resulting in more products produced, and better on-time performance. What's interesting is that Alex doesn't even have to keep everyone busy to succeed.

It's the same with remote management: Evaluating the number of hours someone sits on his butt and types does not equal productivity. It's nice to see people arriving and leaving on time. It's nice to see people typing and working. But sometimes it's the guy who annoys management by showing up at all sorts of weird hours who produces the most. As we've learned, an average worker is only productive for two hours and fifty-three minutes in an eight-hour shift. So, if we can't measure time, what can we measure? And along the same line of questions: What is the bottleneck? what we should be measuring is the output, the amount of work produced, and the bottleneck, in this case is the distraction.

Evaluating work and dealing with distractions are, without a doubt, the scariest parts of management. Notice I said management, not just remote management. But, of course, these challenges will be even harder with remote workers. Also, when I say evaluating work, I'm not only referring to the quality of effort, but whether a job is done within a reasonable amount of time.

It is important that most managers be experts in their fields. In a software company, a manager should be an expert coder. In a recruitment company like DistantJob, the manager needs to climb the ranks of the company by being a great recruiter — or at least be solicited from another excellent recruitment job.

But what if this isn't the case? Let me assure you, this is not hypothetical. Managers are sometimes not experts in their field. Rather, they get promoted based on other talents, such as motivating people or creating great team culture. How do you handle that situation? Well, let me get personal here.

When I was at my first company, Empire Host, I managed a group of system administrators. Unfortunately, I did not have much experience in fixing servers, and I remember it being a major handicap. With DistantJob, the company I run now, it's the opposite. In the beginning, I was doing all the recruitment myself. I was filtering people through chat at an intense speed by talking to two, three, even five people at the same time. So, at Empire Host, I was under-qualified in evaluating the time and effort needed to do the job. But at DistantJob, I had a more luxurious problem of being overqualified. Because of that, I simply could not expect people to work at my pace, so I had no idea what a reasonable amount of effort was. Well, to be frank, at Empire Host, I just struggled with challenges and hoped that my managers were doing their jobs right, which was not the healthiest strategy. At DistantJob, I now have a grip on how to do it right. Here's how I did it:

When it comes to recruitment, you could evaluate your team based on the number of quality candidates they bring in. The problem is that there are often too many moving parts to truly analyze the effort based on this goal. Sometimes you can land on a quality person by mistake on your first try, and sometimes you can be stuck in the middle of a pandemic, where no quality people want to transition from their existing jobs. So in order to break down the process in a more scientific way, we analyze how many people your team has attempted to contact. Then in order to qualify it even more, we look at how many people have responded back.

These two main measurements are called the KPI (key performance indicators). To understand the effectiveness of your team's effort, you must first evaluate the KPI in the most scientific way possible. With proper software and tracking data, we are able to evaluate the amount of outreach and response which is happening on a daily basis. Now, once we figure out the appropriate KPI, the bigger challenge becomes how to find out what kinds of numbers make a reasonable KPI. The good news is that for many who are using Agile methodologies such as Scrum, a manager doesn't necessarily have to figure this out by himself.

So how does Agile work? During the first meeting of each week (also known as the sprint meeting), the team starts providing its expectations and goals for the week. As a manager, you would hope that those estimations aren't too conservative. Of course, adding a little somethin' somethin' to the mix like a nice commission and promotion opportunities wouldn't hurt. If you're thinking about putting something on their pillow, please don't...we don't believe in negative reinforcement. If this doesn't work too well, you will just have to wait a bit till you grow, and hopefully, hire more senior people. These people will see the bar is set, and they'll want to prove themselves. With a little basic peer pressure, the team will start motivating and pushing each other to set bigger goals. When an Agile system works well, a manager's job is not to set even higher goals but rather to make sure that no one gets burned out.

Eventually a manager will get to see what's considered to be a reasonable maximum output while keeping employees happy and motivated. The key is to make sure there is a proper tracking system, so that it's easy to define measurable goals. At DistantJob when we started setting up proper goals with proper measuring systems, we were better able to understand what to expect from our recruiters. Alternatively, you can hire an outside consultant to define expectations — but even then, this can only happen if there's a proper tracking system in place. Even in tough industries like coding, a non-programmer manager can learn if his team is producing quality work. It always goes back to evaluating the KPIs.

TAKEAWAY:

In a remote work environment it's even more important to understand how much your company produces. To do that, you must build a system that lets you calculate the effort and success of your team (KPI). Then you can use your team, outside experts, and your expertise to evaluate optimal output.

II - CREATING TRUST IN A REMOTE WORLD

One of the major concerns with badly managed remote staff is that they can disappear into what I call the Remote Lalaland. It's a very strange place, where workers wake up in the morning, brush their teeth, sit in front of their computers and get to work. Actually that sounds pretty good, right? But a badly managed or ill-fitting remote worker won't particularly care about the effect their work has on the company or if their work has any impact. They simply want to get paid so they can pay their bills. This is usually the result of two factors. The first is the possibility that the person was wrongly hired for the job and didn't fit the job requirement or culture. A more common reason is that management failed to establish the proper level of communication and trust to engage with the person. When it comes to your remote team, you must open these lines of communication and make sure that people feel like they still have a team to work with. Below are some issues that you need to address in order to achieve this level of trust.

Consistency

Managing people from afar can get very messy if the management team provides a bunch of different messages. As I mentioned a few times in this book, being a good remote manager means being a good manager in general; while you can't get away with losing trust in an office environment, in a virtual office the importance of trust becomes even more crucial. The perfect way to lose that trust is by providing inconsistent messages.

If you say one day that there are no stupid questions and no consequences for asking any question, then the next day you shout at a team member for asking *a stupid question*, you are killing trust and hurting their ability to produce. If you do that in front of other people, the damage multiplies across the company.

As another example, if you ask your coders to provide notes in a certain way and then get upset over redundant notes, you are killing the trust of your people and hurting their ability to produce. I'm not saying that you can't change your mind. You are allowed to improve the processes, just be clear and polite about it. I truly hope that most managers in your company understand the difference between sounding crazy and providing productive change. If they don't, you should call them out on it.

Now, it doesn't matter if you are the big boss or a lower-level manager. To get consistency right, make sure that the rest of the management team is on the same wavelength. That's why defining processes and clarifying the company's culture can be a huge advantage for everyone and should be repeated and clarified across the company. Consistency truly makes you look and sound less like an asshole.

> **TAKEAWAY:**
>
> **Try to follow the values you define in your company; if you have to change something about those values, do so mindfully. It's important to have your entire team on the same wavelength.**

Build An Asshole-Free Environment

I don't know if you've noticed a common theme in this book, but it's pretty simple, really: Being an asshole is bad for business — remote, or otherwise.

The days of asshole bosses are coming to an end. It is unfortunate that management by fear still works sometimes. But with modern technologies and a stronger focus on quality service, this management style is slowly dying out.

In 2007, a book dedicated to this topic was written by a Stamford University professor named Robert I. Sutton. In his book, Sutton describes how an *asshole environment* drastically increases staff turnover. For those who stick around, anxiety levels are high, depression rampant, and burnout, which of course affects the bottom line, is a real problem.

A British study referenced in this book showed that when people see a manager behave like an asshole to an employee, 73 percent become significantly more stressed, and 44 percent expect to be the next victim. There is also research out of the UK showing that 25 percent of people who are bullied in an office environment, and 20 percent of people who witness the bullying (which is a ratio of two witnesses per one victim) leave the company. Combining these numbers with consideration that 15% of workers in the UK have experienced bullying means that about 97 people leave an office of 1000. This equates to nearly $2 million in replacement costs.

In other words, being a dick costs a lot of money.

If working with assholes causes damage in the physical world, in the virtual world those damages can become outright disasters. In a world where you depend on people to be a bit more motivated and independent—in a world that it is somewhat easier to cheat the system and that much harder to track—very few factors can kill productivity faster than an asshole at the helm.

TAKEAWAY:

Being a dick causes stress, burnout, and lower retention, which ends up costing your company a lot of money. Don't be a dick.

Building Trust

Communication is everything in a remote working environment. When you don't see your staff every day, understanding what they are doing becomes vital. Again, these are skills that are also crucial in a local office. But in a remote environment, you just can't survive without communication.

Yet in order to achieve real communication, you must build trust. Now, the trust that I'm referring to is not the trust that involves you believing that the person you are dealing with is honest, nor is it believing that the person is competent enough or has enough experience to achieve the goal. Don't get me wrong, these are important attributes to have, but I'm talking about a different kind of trust.

I'm talking about the trust that you create within your company—a trust that lets people on your team communicate with you about everything. If George Lucas had this kind of trust with his employees, they wouldn't have created this awful, awful prequel to Star Wars. (Sorry, that was a bit of nerdy anger.) This trust is knowing that your employees will call you out on your shit, that they will not accept your word as the word of some know-it-all guru.

You *need* your team to challenge you and engage in constructive conflict. As a manager or a boss, you need to ask yourself, if someone calls you an asshole or suggests you're incompetent in some capacity, how do you handle it? If you want to learn *why* the person feels this way, you are in a good place. If you fire the person on the spot, you will never have trust.

And for those of you who don't understand what I mean by constructive conflict, it is passionately arguing about a constructive topic, without getting personal or taking it personally. (A skill that we clearly don't gain from Facebook). Constructive conflict is not only important for the boss/employee relationship, it is how people get real opinions from each other. If you don't get a bit angry sometimes, if you don't challenge ideas hard enough, then you are not going to get strong ideas from your team. Once you have trust, solid communication is possible. And, getting this trust can only start from the top.

If you are the owner or president of your company, start with a lot of disclaimers. Make it clear that you are genuinely open to communication within your ranks. Don't expect instant success, but if you make it clear that it is your responsibility to create trust, you'll get more traction. If your staff start seeing this in action, where your senior team members tell you what is on their mind without holding back, that will build this trust in a big way. You must also do it in reverse. Hold people accountable when they could have communicated with you on a key topic but didn't, while rewarding people who do a great job of communicating and challenging you.

Of course, you must deliver on that trust and avoid shutting down people's honest opinions. If you don't have the time or patience for someone, just politely tell them that you are sorry but unfortunately, it's not the right time. Even if it's coming from that annoying rookie who hasn't yet gotten a chance to learn anything but already has 10 million opinions, manage it politely, because others are listening. Remember, if one time you put down a person for challenging you, you could lose three months of trust-building efforts. If you do that in front of a group, you will lose the same amount of time for the entire group.

So, if you are having a bad day, be honest about it. Let people know that unless it's urgent it's not the right time to talk. Actually even better, talk to as few people as possible. No one needs to chat with Captain Rage and no one cares that you binged the last season of *How I Met Your Mother* and had to endure that awful ending. If you screw up and come across as a dick, apologize, and be sincere. It simply goes back to that basic concept: No assholes allowed.

Just to note, I'm a true believer that a great leader does not need to be the smartest guy in the room; it's very much a good thing if your team surpasses you on most of your skills. Yet, it's completely pointless to have a smart team if they don't trust you or each other, and as a result avoid saying what's on their mind.

TAKEAWAY:

You must gain your employees' trust, so that they can say what's on their mind without any consequences. You win that trust by showing that even pointed criticism of their managers will have no consequences, as long as that criticism is constructive.

Mistake-Friendly Environment

Honestly, I wish I could tell you that I have built my company strictly on the advice of others. I do ask for advice and study and read a lot. But unfortunately, and too often, I just grind through mistakes. As my dad used to tell me, "Your mistakes will cost you a lot of money. But so does an Ivy League education."

If you want your employees to be independent and think outside the box, create an environment that encourages these traits. If you want your staff to stop nagging you with very obvious questions, make your office a mistake-friendly environment. This is kind of an extension of building trust and creating an asshole-free environment. Only this time, instead of building trust so your employees can tell you anything and challenge you with any idea you have, this is building trust so your employees can feel comfortable experimenting without consequences.

In a remote environment, you want your people to be independent. So just as you would reward staff for challenging you and calling you out, reward them for taking risks and trying things that could go wrong. Set a budget limit for how much people can spend and a time limit for how much they can devote to their risky ventures. Let's not be confused here, you still want to hear about the experiment, but treat everything as an experiment. If you're anything like me, you simply don't understand any other way to grow, so why would I expect any different from my people?

If you want independent workers, invest in their independence. Let them make mistakes.

TAKEAWAY:

Encourage people to make mistakes and learn from them.

Avoiding cliques in a hybrid environment

Loneliness or mental health challenges aren't the sole factors that threaten employee motivation while remote. Some highly productive employees can lose motivation due to hybrid work environments.

Let me explain what a hybrid environment is. As I write this in the summer of 2020, many companies have sent most (and in many cases, all) of their people home. While that transition creates some logistical challenges to make it happen, there's also a lot less conflict in terms of managing your people. A more interesting challenge will be once the pandemic eases, your company is ready to resume in-person work, and you face the decision of whether or not to leave certain people to work from home, because they really enjoy the experience and thrive in that environment. Once you understand how to manage those new remote workers, you might even start hiring some people internationally.

This is what we call a hybrid work environment, where some people work from home and some work from the office. This creates a few challenges in terms of communication, motivation, running meetings, and office politics. One of the biggest challenges with a hybrid environment is that the people who are in the office often get information first, and almost always connect better with their colleagues. As a manager, you must fight this. You must make sure that your remote people always get informed on time, or sometimes even before your local ones. You must do everything in your power to level the playing field. If you don't, your company will eventually become a clique for local employees vs. remote.

Although there are many wonderful tools for using in a conference room as we will discuss in the technology section, having seven local employees sitting in the same room and then one other employee sitting somewhere else is not a way to make the remote person feel that her input is equal. So how do you fight this? Some experts say that a hybrid remote/local company should be managed as if *everyone* is remote. We call this the *"One remote, all remote"* policy.

Don't even use a conference room. Just put everyone on Zoom equally and voila, no more cliques. In one of the following sections of this book we will explore how remote collaborative brainstorming can be awesome. If you don't want to put too much thinking into this and your team already enjoys working with Slack and project management software, then why not just do that? Honestly, some companies are so big that actually going to meet with each other two floors below is a waste of time, so they might as well consider everyone remote. Yet for some of us this might be overkill.

In certain creative companies it's really nice to hang out with people physically while coming up with solutions, and you wouldn't necessarily want to lose that energy. If that's the case, you must have the best conference tools. You might even need to add a telepresence robot or two. And you must check all the time that the information reaches the remote people as quickly as it does local people. When it comes to big announcements, I recommend that you make them online, so that everyone feels on the same page at the same time. You simply do not want a local vs. remote battle royale. Both groups should appreciate each other, and if there is some concern over jealousy, send them home (or vice versa) to experience how their counterparts feel.

III - DISTRACTIONS

Considering that every company's goal is to produce, the biggest enemy of productivity is not fewer hours, or even less training. It's distraction. Well actually, it's a lack of skills, but we will have to assume that our readers hire at least semi-competent people...in which case distraction becomes the biggest concern.

In an office environment, a person gets distracted every 11 minutes (on average). Considering it takes a person 25 minutes to get their brain back on task after a distraction, I don't even see how we manage to get those two hours and fifty-three minutes of productive time in per day.

During a crisis, if you have to work from home and can't find anything exciting about the change, at least you can get excited about reducing distractions. That is, of course, if you don't have a toddler (and then you are simply doomed, sorry). You have to make sure not to bring home the distractions you might have in an office. Here are a few issues to reflect on:

Meetings

We have sooooooo many meetings. Brainstorming meetings, information-gathering meetings, making decisions meetings, your boss needs to boost his ego meetings, your manager feels insecure about his idea but is not really willing to change his idea meetings, meetings about planning more meetings, meetings to discuss the kinds of meats we want to eat when meeting at meetings.

Unfortunately, if you look at any list of the most distracting activities in an office, meetings usually top that list. According to a Clarizen and Harris Poll[4], the average American employee spends more than nine hours each week preparing for or sitting through meetings. Sixty percent considered meetings to be distractions. You are not only taking people away from their work, you also get them to stop projects in the middle, which takes even more time to come back. Meetings are seldom productive. There are usually a few people that take charge and quite a few others who are not interested in being there and have nothing to contribute. Especially in the tech world it

---

4   https://www.clarizen.com/press-release/clarizen-survey-workers-consider-status-meetings-a-productivity-killing-waste-of-time/

is common to see people coming to a meeting with the laptop acting like they are paying attention but still doing their work in a half-assed way.

There is no question that meeting strategies have to improve in general. But when it comes to working with remote staff, having too many people in a meeting is not only unproductive, it even hinders the few people who are actually contributing.

Unfortunately, even the popular Zoom app does not give you the same fluid experience that you get in a physical experience. For example, if you celebrated Easter or Passover during the coronavirus pandemic with your family, you know how challenging that was. And the grandparents—oh, the grandparents. I still cringe at my father whispering to my mother during the Passover meal, "how wonderful technology is today," not understanding that everyone can hear him. Followed by my mom's phone ringing and my mom not knowing that the sound would ring in everyone's ears. I think there should be a new rule that grandparents are not allowed to use Zoom until they learn how to use the mute button.

But grandparents are not the only ones having a hard time with big groups. In conferencing software, sound simply does not transfer as well as it does in a physical conference room. So, going remote is a good time to cut the frequency of your meetings, or at least the number of people in them. Finally you won't feel the pressure to fill up all the empty seats in your conference room.

Just to be clear, I'm not saying to avoid meetings entirely. But I do feel that they need to be done responsibly. Which means, don't invite people who don't need to be there and make sure that the meeting is not just paying lip service, but actually creating ideas and actionable tasks. At DistantJob, I started a new policy. After defining a meeting's goals beforehand, any team member who does not feel he will benefit from the meeting can opt out without penalty.

Ask yourself if you need all of those meetings. Brainstorming meetings are important. Getting your team on the same page is also incredibly important, especially in a remote environment. Do an honest audit. If you think the meeting has no point, get rid of it.

TAKEAWAY:

Pay attention to any meeting that might not be useful. Long and frequent meetings are an incredible distraction, so focus on reducing their length and frequency.

Chats

Another offender is cubicles—not just cubicles but any close working environments. We sit people in cubicles and think this will create better dynamics, but what we are actually doing is creating distractions. A distraction can come from a well-meaning buddy who wants to discuss the latest COVID-19 news, or an awesome Netflix show he saw last night. It could be the lady two cubicles down talking to a client over the telephone or that annoying guy who keeps flirting with the secretary.

According to a 2016 survey by CareerBuilder[5], the second-biggest distraction in an office, after browsing the Internet, is gossip; 39 percent of respondents listed idle chatter as an office distraction. Research from Ipsos shows that overall, 87% percent of people are dissatisfied with their work environment, because they can't concentrate. This is a real and scary statistic[6].

Now, you're probably reading this and wondering, "Come on Sharon, I'm at home, I don't have anyone to bother. There are no cubicles and there are no colleagues, so why are we worried about this?"

---

5   http://press.careerbuilder.com/2016-06-08-New-CareerBuilder-Survey-Reveals-How-Much-Smartphones-Are-Sapping-Productivity-at-Work

6   http://cdn2.hubspot.net/hubfs/1822507/2016-WPR/Americas/Final_Digital_PDF.pdf

Well, unfortunately, there's Slack and Google Hangouts and Skype, and any one of these apps can bring the office gossiper to your home computer. Chat programs and instant messaging tools—when used inefficiently—can mimic an office environment in some of the worst ways, and prove to be just as distracting.

Now that buddy of yours can talk about COVID-19 and Netflix through text. Even worse, your boss can randomly and effortlessly page you via Skype and expect an immediate response. It does not mean that Slack can't be an amazing tool, but it's important to use digital communication tools very carefully.

When DistantJob started growing and I started dealing with quite a few more employees, I remember we used to use MSN Messenger back then. I would never put myself in away mode because I was always happy to respond to anyone. I would wake up every morning and message everyone, "Hi." Simply the word "Hi," nothing else. For me, "Hi" meant, *Hey I'm around, do you want to chat?*

But later on, when I finally gained enough trust from my employees to tell me the truth, I saw this from a different perspective. "Hi," to my staff, meant something completely different. To them, it meant, *Holy cow, my boss just messaged me. I have no idea what he wants so I'd better stop everything that I'm doing and reply. I hope it's nothing bad. For them it was, "Hi," as in, are you doing something productive?* Man, it's pretty amazing how far an innocent "Hi" can go. I was only trying to replicate what I had learned to be standard office manager practice. It was the virtual equivalent of going from one desk to another, checking on my people, helping them, answering questions, and providing motivation. But what I was actually doing was continuously distracting my employees and making them anxious.

When I was asking them to do something, I didn't realize that I was stopping them from finishing the project they were working on. It was creating an unproductive environment.

So through the years, I learned a few solid lessons about controlling chatter:

1. Build trust within your company, so people can tell you when they are busy or unable to take on a discussion or project.

2. Implement project management software that tracks what your employees are doing, and lets them update you in between projects. This way you can keep track of their effort without distracting them.

3. We encourage people to put themselves in away or non-distraction mode and not to

worry if they miss someone's message. If there is an important message that needs immediate attention, we encourage them to use this strange app that's foreign to many millennials and Gen-Z types...it's called a phone. An actual phone that you use to call people, not one built solely for Tinder and Candy Crush. We also dedicated an app called Telegram as the chat solution you can use in urgent situations. That way you have to keep your mobile phone on, but use your mobile sparingly and Telegram respectfully.

4. In general, chat software is not made to nudge people to start a conversation; it's made to get to the point. So when you're asking for someone's attention clearly, define what it is that you want to discuss. No random Hi's, ever!

TAKEAWAY:

Instant messaging/chat software can be great tools to for communicating remotely. They are also the perfect tools to create distractions. Use responsibly.

Regular check-ins

OK, so some of you have the luxury to sit in an office with a closed door. There is great sound isolation and you don't hear anyone unless you want to. With a nice office like that, you probably hold a senior position in the company. I guess you are immune to distractions, right? Wrong. Working in a closed room might take away the background noise, but it doesn't prevent people from constantly barging in, checking on you, or asking you questions. I remember a long time ago when I actually had employees sitting with me in the office, one of them was the company's accountant who came into the office only once a week. She took care of invoices and billing and assisted both the candidates and the clients with their financial issues. She did a great job and truly helped me keep the company afloat. So, the day she did not work from home, she regularly came to my room to check in and ask questions.

Often, I found myself frustrated with her, and I didn't know why. Later on, I realized that while we took care of all her accounting needs, I hardly got any other work done when she was in. When I learned about the 25-minutes rule, everything became clear. She would literally come to my room every half an hour to ask me questions, to the point that it became a parody of a terrible episode of *The Office*. I would start in the morning, sit down, take off my jacket, turn on the computer, do a little stretch, start typing...and two minutes later she would show up with questions. Once we were done, I would sit again, check my emails, type something on Facebook and get to work again...and she'd appear again with another question. Once it was done, I would sit down, check if anyone replied to my Facebook, check a few more emails and she would show again with more questions. And that is how the rest of the day would go. I would think I could recover and get some real work done between her accounting questions, but that was never the reality.

This entire experience made me reflect on how distracting I could be to other people. Looking back, one of the biggest victims was my brother. To his great disappointment, he worked in the same building as me. For at least a decade I kept popping in with jokes and pranks, pulling his focus away from his work. I remember one day when my brother decided to work from home, but he was accessing his office computer using VPN software called GoToMyPC. I happened to be in the office, so I decided to sneak into his room and move his mouse every time he was about to click something. For 10 minutes he thought the VPN was haunted by a ghost virus. It was only later, when I turned on Microsoft Word and started typing "Redrum Redrum Redrum" that he figured out what was going on. Then came a phone call with him shouting at me while I laughed and laughed and laughed, until he eventually had no choice but to join the laughter. I don't regret good pranks, but now I realize that this prank cost him an hour of focused effort. So if you choose to prank someone at work, make sure it's worth it, and make sure that it's a short prank.

On a more serious note, at DistantJob, my vice president burned out for a short while. The reason why? He kept an open-door policy all day, every day, and couldn't get things done when staff popped into his office at all hours. Together we learned so much about the power of distraction at all levels of the company.

Unless you get to a stage where teaching, motivating, and fixing issues are all you do every day, having staff pop into your office every few minutes is incredibly distracting. You need to create a plan to combat this cycle. As a manager you need to define your open hours (whether in person or remote), and make sure your employees respect those boundaries.

TAKEAWAY:

It's hard to get work done with an unlimited open-door policy. Manage your schedule so that you can take care of your employees' needs while still maintaining productive time for yourself.

Tech And Social Media

Today, with the migration toward working from home, you can get rid of bad office habits while implementing good remote habits. Unfortunately, some of the common distractions such as phone games and social media can be more challenging in remote environments, because you don't even need to put up that fake Excel sheet anytime a manager passes by to cover your tracks.

I highly recommend you purchase app blockers such as SelfControl or RescueTime for your team members and let them use it at the own discretion. You can laugh all you want about self-restricting apps, but they shockingly work. Many of you can cheat or hack them, but the few minutes that it takes you to create the loophole is all the time your brain needs to take over and understand that you are going in the wrong direction, toward being devoured by social media and online gaming addiction.

If one of your team members has chosen to use a self-restricting app themselves, don't mock them, and don't use that as an opportunity to find out what they did before. Instead, reward them for taking such an initiative.

> ## TAKEAWAY:
>
> **If you are worried that your team is wasting too much time on social media and gaming, buy them app blockers to help them better manage their time.**

House and family

Even a home can come with its own distractions. Sometimes the laundry calls or the backyard pool looks enticing. The fridge continuously talks to me. "Sharrrrroooonnn, come to me, I've got a sandwich for you. Sharrrrooon I have ice cream with your name on it. It's the one that merges salty caramel with dark fudge, come to the dark side."

Working from home takes discipline. Sometimes daycare is closed, schools are closed, and the babysitter is not available. At this very moment while trying to write this book my little one is trying to pick my nose. I keep telling her that you can pick your friends, and you can pick your nose, but you can't pick your friend's nose.

This is not just a pandemic thing. Life constantly throws us curveballs. Taking care of older parents, sick kids, a spouse who needs your help, the list goes on and on.

The best thing you can do as a manager is to keep an open discussion with your staff, so that they feel supported during these times. Come up with coping strategies together, and respect that they might have challenges during times of crisis. Depending on the budget, you might be able to help your employees by helping them pay for childcare. You can work with a catering service to deliver food, or send them a cleaning lady to help around the house. These are all legitimate business expenses that can help your remote employees feel less distracted and more productive, making them potentially valuable investments.

Unfortunately, you can't fix all of your employees' time-consuming life challenges. But you can definitely buy them time by removing at-home chores and tasks that can get in the way of their work. You can also guide them or offer them a coach on how to be more productive at home, even with tons of distractions around. Being patient and helpful through challenging times will help you create incredibly loyal employees.

TAKEAWAYS:

Be understanding and patient. Your employees will remember that forever.

If budget permits, try to pay for services that address your employees' time-consuming chores, reducing their distractions and freeing up more time for them to be productive.

The Whatchamacallit Effect

These days, I find more and more people who actually get it. They understand the need to replicate the office experience at home, without going too far. They take care of their staff's mental health and wellbeing, offer help to avoid distractions, and treat their remote staff with respect. Still, every once in a while, I get feedback from a client or potential client who still finds that a remote or partly remote setup isn't working for their company. They can't put their finger on *why*, but they know they don't have the same relationship with their remote staff that they have with someone sitting in their office.

I call this unknown experience the whatchamacallit effect.

I've spent a long time searching for this great unknown, evaluating my experience, asking colleagues questions, and interviewing clients. I think I finally discovered what this whatchamacallit effect is. It's made up from small irritants that you are not entirely aware of, but still get to you on a subconscious level.

When trying to communicate with remote workers, you may experience a strange background noise, an echo, seeing a person in the dark, a delayed response, or sometimes the inability to understand what the person is saying. This effect makes you exhausted without knowing it. It is a combination of latency, poor audio quality and video quality.

I initially understood it with my super awesome brother, who is somewhat sensitive to sound. I could see that whenever we used a mediocre digital communication tool, he started to get a bit frustrated. When I sat in front of him to hang out, we never had an issue—not only because he had a beer in his hand, but because his ears and his eyes are built for the real world. When you use a webcam, a phone, or any other communication tool, you don't get the same experience as the real world. Digital technology has a much harder time filtering background noise and also prevents our ears from filtering noise.

The same goes for the visual. Our eyes do an incredible job adjusting to darker scenery, but a camera does not capture or interpret light the same way. So, darker light that is easy for the eyes to capture in real life can make a person look really shadowy and unapproachable on video. It's pretty crazy how many times I have to chat with Captain Mysterio.

The biggest micro offender is latency. If you've ever made a joke on a webcam and your friend kept his straight face like he completely did not understand that you even made a joke, only to start laughing uncontrollably a few seconds later, you've experienced the annoyance of latency. It's even worse in a constructive conflict where everyone is trying to make a point, but no one knows when the other person finishes. It's like talking on an old-school walkie-talkie where you need to say *over* after you finish every phrase to get the conversation moving forward.

While some people are more sensitive than others, hindering fluid communication can eventually frustrate anyone. Based on the horrible whatchamacallit effect, you may end up subconsciously or even consciously resenting your online discussion. This in turn can make you think twice before going online. And when you avoid online conversation altogether, you experience communication death, which is also the death of the entire remote experience.

Do not fear. Minimal technology upgrades can solve the whatchamacallit effect.

In simple terms, buy your employees a quality headset. Stick with trusted brands like Plantronics and Jabra, which focus on communication and have powerful noise-canceling microphones. Invest in a light filter, and for crying out loud, don't skimp on the Internet. Always get two versions better than what you would expect to be the right speed, and invest in great routers.

If I'm not stating the obvious, when you are having a meeting with your team, make it clear that coffee shops and other noisy environments are not the best places for people to work. As a boss who preaches remote, I try hard to be cool with the working environment of choice. Clearly, a coffee shop is a cool place to work, but my whatchamacallit radar hits level 10 when I chat with someone in one of those environments. Quite frankly, I'm also not convinced that distractions can be well managed in those types of places.

These small steps could eliminate most of your minimal distractions and get you a truly real-time experience as if you are talking to someone in the next cubicle.

TAKEAWAY:

Pay attention to small annoyances in your virtual discussions. They can drastically hurt the experience and may exhaust you to the point that you might want to reduce communication. A bit of an upgrade in technology can solve all that.

IV - Technology

Alright, so we started discussing tech in the previous chapter, and how important it is to make these small investments in technology. Investing in technology changes the entire remote relationship, and as we learned in the previous chapter, the level of satisfaction with the conversation. To be clear, when you invest in the right technology, one of your biggest goals is to make sure the person sitting across the world from you feels like he is sitting in your office.

So here's what to look for.

Video

We are quite a few years away from a completely interactive experience like a hologram, and it doesn't seem like we are ready to start putting on virtual reality headsets every time we want to talk to someone. But by purchasing a quality camera like the Logitech C920 series or the Logitech C930, you'll get the quality you need. Yet in reality, it is rarely the webcam that causes a bottleneck, and if it is, it's because of the amount of light in the room. As in photography, purchasing an inexpensive LED light or webcam light ring can make a huge difference. You can find these on Amazon for under fifty bucks, and remember to keep the light in front of you, not at your back. There is even a great webcam called the Razer Kiyo that comes with a light on it.

Also, for the interactive manager who likes to pace the room, Facebook has created a new cam called Portal. This piece of hardware is really cool, bringing visual interactivity to the next level. Portal is a wide-angle webcam that follows you across the room. It zooms in and zooms out based on where you are, so you can freely roam anywhere you want in the room, and the camera will see you. The only disadvantage is that you can't talk in your underwear.

I have to say that the idea of getting anything from Facebook makes me cringe considering their privacy track record. Then again if you use Alexa, Google Nest, or any device form a multinational company that is giving you things for free or nearly free, you probably lost the privacy battle a long time ago.

Voice

It continuously surprises me that the biggest brands in headphones can't come up with a quality communication device that incorporates a great microphone into a great headset. So, whatever you do, don't jump to get the latest Bose, Beats, or Sony headset. They all suck. Plantronics and Jabra are the true brands of communication, and whether you find these an eyesore or not, no technology gets it right without a directional microphone. Yes, this includes your Apple AirPods.

You still need the microphone to be in front of your face to get the quality of sound you want. Unfortunately, they have not yet created the perfect headset, where it is all at once visually appealing and comfortable, with full over-the-ear pads that are breathable and don't overheat your ears, sound good for both speech and music, has an exceptional microphone, Bluetooth that does not get distorted, and an easy-to-use docking station. (Get on this, techies!!)

Yes, this is my dream headset, and it does not exist. But while I wait, I find myself enjoying the Jabra Evolve 75, which is a Bluetooth headset. Wired headsets are still much better than wireless models, considering the Bluetooth interruptions and battery life. For those concerned with the headset messing up their hair, there is also the Jabra Evolve 75e, which sits on your neck. Whatever you do, don't compromise on quality when it comes to headsets. You can also use a high-quality microphone USB microphone, like the Yeti.

The other key piece of technology for smooth conversation is your Internet connection. Considering we all live in different places, I can't recommend a specific brand for Internet access. Unfortunately, no matter where you are, your choices probably consist of massive conglomerates that offer horrible service; even when you do find a smaller company with better service, it might be a reseller of the same big company you dread.

The way to do this is to upgrade your Internet until you stop noticing interruptions, skips, and latencies, then go two or three versions better. It usually ends up costing more per month, but that higher level of service changes everything. Speeds that far surpass your requirements help with latencies, especially these days when everyone is clogging the Internet. If you want to get a bit more technical, spend time going to every room in your house and search for areas where the WiFi is not working well with an app called WiFi Analyzer. You can also test your Internet speed by going to speedtest.net.

As of this writing in the summer of 2020, you should be fine with a 50MBPS upload and download, and you don't need to go over 100MBPS. If your Internet is the right speed but you found dead or weak zones, consider investing in stronger routers or even better mesh network routers, which mean two or more identical routers that distribute your Internet properly across a bigger area. I was blown away when I purchased my Netgear Orbi. Not only could I reach my backyard and the deepest part of my basement at 600MBPS, but the Internet was six times faster and more stable even in the room of the original router.

To make your team feel connected, make sure your VOIP (Voice Over IP) system has all the features that make them feel like they are in the same office, even the ability to use a landline phone. At DistantJob, we use RingCentral cloud-based communications technology to its full capacity; it gives each one of us an extension and phone number. So when a client calls our office, our assistant picks up the phone and easily transfers or conferences anyone within seconds. No one even knows we are not a physical office unless we tell them.

Such a simple investment can make your staff feel more professional, and let your customers know they're in good hands.

Conferencing and Chat Software

Let's talk software—conferencing software, specifically. Today, Zoom is leading the pack for a reason. Even before Zoom became such a hit, we tested 10 different platforms and found Zoom to be the best. It not only provided great streaming, it's also incredibly easy to use, which proved to be the most important attribute of conference software.

Without shaming other apps, before Zoom every time I invited someone to an interview, connecting took several minutes and did not work on every operating system. For most, a different operating system is not a huge deal, but in the nerd world you continuously get people connecting from different Linux distributions. Being able to provide a link so the other person is online in a few seconds is amazing for that real-time experience you want to achieve.

One of my favorite features is the Zoom shortcut in Slack, where I don't need to go to the app and set up a meeting. I just type /zoom and a link pops up for everyone to join. Nothing spells a real interactive non-big brother experience better than "Hey, come talk to me," and the person is on camera within seconds.

And there's your easy segue to Slack. Slack is a real-time chat software platform, and I like it for the exact same reason I like Zoom: ease of use. It is easy to start a new chat, set up groups, and share files. There are many great plugins like Giphy to bring humor to conversations and Donut to create one-on-one personal meetings so the group can get to know each other. Of course, my favorite is the Zoom plugin that I mentioned above. Slack is expensive for what it does, and I might search for an alternative in the future. But you couldn't ask for an easier piece of software to use if you have a healthy budget.

Project Management Software

Project management software is key for remote management. It's a way to track and document everything that is happening across the company. It's the way you track progress not just for projects but also daily tasks and goals. If you create solid onboarding from the beginning and don't forget to put emphasis on social connection, you can practically run the entire company through this software.

Picking your management software is not as straightforward and clear-cut as other tech-related investments for your business. It is totally based on the way you manage, brainstorm, and track your work and management processes. You will have to do a lot of experimenting, and I'm talking from experience. At DistantJob, we heavily tested multiple project management tools, going back and forth several times, so we can give you some suggestions.

With today's momentum towards remote hiring, managing, and working, everyone wants to climb aboard the remote train. Remote is becoming a buzzword, same as "cloud" and "cryptocurrency", and software companies are getting involved. Cut through the noise, and it's fair to say that only one company has truly built its software with remote management in mind. Basecamp is not only software that's great for remote work; the company's entire operation is remote, so Basecamp was able to build and test it themselves. Basecamp is, without a doubt, old-school software with some pretty outdated interactive experiences. But it created an environment where remote staff could show their progress without distractions, a hugely important tool for any company working with a remote staff.

Features like written daily standups are an alternative for the Scrummers (people who use Scrum technology) who are used to physical meetings. For us at DistantJob, managing distraction and organizing tasks are key features. Basecamp comes at a great price per month and allows unlimited users, which is amazing.

The other tools we have heavily tested are Asana and Trello. Here's the feedback my VP gave on Trello:

"Trello's biggest plus is its out-of-the-box simplicity. It is a straight forward tool that is easy to work with. You almost don't need an intro, especially if you know how to work with the management methodology called Kanban. Trello is essentially a Kanban board, and you should treat it like one. You can quickly see an overview of how your current project is moving if you follow the onboard principles. The best use of Trello is as a tool for Kanban."

Trello is great when you have a pipeline process. At DistantJob, we use it for content creation. We follow through the writing stages, and when the Kanban setup is right, you have a good throughput. Unfortunately, it gets quite tedious to set things up when you have complicated tasks to deal with. It's not useful when your projects are too complex. The more complexity you add, the more magic you kill. There is no proper overview of projects.

Another system we used was Asana. What makes Asana great is you can customize it, adapting it to different types of workflow. It's a more complicated system that allows you to build your projects according to your needs. Unlike Trello, Asana enables you to build and handle complex projects. The main dashboard gives you a better look at ongoing projects. Asana offers a free version with a lot of limitations. It's great, but it makes you work for it; you need to learn the software to use it to its full extent. It takes time and effort to learn.

Asana is not as intuitive as Trello and isn't as enjoyable to use. But Asana is far more robust and can be tailored to much more complex projects, once you get the hang of it.

Equipping Your Physical Conference Room

The physical conference room is controversial. In many companies, the room is full of chairs that can make the manager feel like she needs to fill them. But now, when integrating remote people, it becomes an entirely different monster. Some companies simply bring everyone on Zoom, but in some circumstances, this isn't possible. When meetings are a mix of physical team members and remote team members, aim for a proper ratio. Don't leave your virtual participants on those absolutely awful speakerphones, since those speakers will make them feel like outsiders. If you want your conference room to be a comfortable space for all, consider robust technological options.

Of course, visuals matter a lot. People need to see each other. If you use Zoom, use a big screen to show everyone's face. Arrange the room so the team members present sit in a semi-circle that includes the screen.

You can also use a telepresence robot like Kubi. Well, to call Kubi a robot is an exaggeration. It's actually a tablet on a moving arm you control. When positioned where a person would sit, the virtual team member feels like she's there in the boardroom. How cool is that? You can also use technological tools like an Owl webcam, which is a revolving cam that can move to see anyone in the room.

You can also take things to the next level. Up to this point I've been talking about how to equip your team with affordable solutions to make the remote experience better. But what if you run a big, highly profitable company that's not looking for affordable solutions, but instead looking to create the ultimate Hybrid experience, where people in the office and people at home work in complete sync?

For that, I welcome you to the future. Introducing Immersive Studio conference rooms, by

Polycom. The Immersive Studio room creates an environment that makes it seem like you and a dozen of your closest work friends are all in the same room, seeing each other and hearing each other talk with perfect clarity. What you get is a series of crisp, clear, individual screens that allow you to see your entire team at one time. Imagine yourself talking to someone on the big screen on the deck of Star Trek's USS Enterprise; that's what Immersive Studio offers.

Having multiple people on separate screens creates the inter-service conference room that truly immerses remote workers into your company culture. And why limit yourself to the conference room? Why not have these screens all over the office, so that remote workers can truly feel like they're walking into someone's office? While today it costs about $100,000 to implement something like this solution, there is no reason to doubt that in the near future we will have apps that can take any smart screen and turn it into an easy communication tool, for not much more than the price of the screen itself. This is truly the future of the hybrid office...at least until the holograms and teleporting machines show up.

Making Working Space Awesome For Your Employees

In Part II, which is about advice for remote workers, we will discuss the importance of creating an amazing working environment. You, as a business owner or manager, can put this responsibility on your employees, or you can own it. You can create a team of happy, content employees by investing in their working environment. I'm not suggesting companies spend a ton of money on technological improvements that aren't necessities, especially when remote work happens due to a crisis or temporary change in business procedures that might hurt your business. In tough times, you need to keep to a budget.

That said, investing in an inexpensive 30-inch screen can make a huge difference. Do you know what pumps people up? Music with bass. Logitech makes great computer speakers that cost less than fast food for four.

Do you want to make your office *cool*? Standing desks run less than a grand, and standing desk converters cost half of that. And, if you want to go crazy, how about a treadmill desk like the Lifespan TR-800? Stay healthy and energized in your work environment.

If your employees are not the getting in shape type, consider getting them a super gaming chair. If they're not gamers but you really want to pamper them, consider providing them with ergonomic office chairs. Find really cool items on Kickstarters and send them to test new, cool products. Or if you are simply out of ideas, just get them a mini-fridge. The amazing thing is that many employees would not feel comfortable having some of these items in a physical office; a standing desk can already feel awkward in a crowded office, a treadmill desk even more so. Pimping your employees' remote offices can ensure they never miss their company office, and that they'll never forget what they company did for them.

V - Protecting your data

So here's the deal. I got this amazing piece of technology which we have been creating inside this building called my office for five years. I know the people who are working on this product, I signed them all to a solid contract where I know where they live and can sue them for every penny they've got. I'm in charge of what will happen to my product. I know everything that happens to my client list. No one can come out of my company using my trade secrets. And if you think that you can ever provide the same type of service after you work for me, you are in for a big surprise.

Don't mess with me! I'm in full control, right?

Right? Anybody???

Well, the answer is yes and no. The laws in the United States are getting stricter to help employers enforce this level of protection that we are talking about. But often companies that are too preoccupied with protecting themselves end up investing tons of resources on this concern while losing focus on what really matters: encouraging quality employees to join your company, and motivating them enough to produce amazing results.

Besides, trying to intimidate your employees will not help you protect your company's assets. To protect your intellectual property, you need solid patents that will need to be constantly defended by an expensive lawyer, not to mention a team of investigators to track the actions of your ex-employees. Because honestly, without safeguards it will be very hard to prevent an ex-employee from transmitting data to another company while acting like they work somewhere else. The closest you can get to true protection is to make sure that your company's data is not transmittable, but like I said that requires an immense amount of resources.

So then if it's so hard to protect your data, trade secrets, and company assets such as client lists from getting leaked by in-person employees, wouldn't it be even harder to protect all this information from remote employees, or even international employees? We are back to the yes and no answer.

Here's an interesting twist: While a person who works from a different state, province, or country will be much harder to catch and expose for a crime, an employee who's not in your office is less likely to have direct contact with your clients, will have fewer chances to mingle with suppliers, and will have less access to files. Think about it this way: If a Nigerian prince ever emails to tell you about his missing fifth toe which made the king disown him, yet somehow he has access to millions in royal money and wants you to help him get out of the country and all he needs is your bank info, social insurance number, death certificate, and credit card, you're more likely to ignore him than you would an in-person grifter. If someone comes to your office in a suit claiming they are from the bank, that you are missing a document, and you must sign on the dotted line, that person has a better chance of successfully scamming you.

Another misconception is that if you need to enforce some kind of contract with international employees, you'll have fewer opportunities to take them to court. I actually find this to be the opposite: If you hire international employees working in countries where the cost of living is lower, top lawyers will be more affordable, and lower-paid workers will be more intimidated to start trouble with a successful company in the western world. So to be clear, the concept of someone remote and international inflicting more damage to your company is false. Again, that's assuming that this is even your priority. I don't put much emphasis on protecting my company from my employees. I would rather put as much faith as I can into their efforts by encouraging and empowering them.

I learned my lesson by spending too much time in the past trying to protect my ideas. I didn't want competitors to run with my ideas for a remote recruitment agency, so I invested a ton of time and energy trying to stay incognito...which was utterly stupid. I have also kept my departments separated, so that the department that was in charge of my clients was completely walled off from the department in charge of finding candidates. I ran it like three different companies: the sales/marketing department when they found a client would immediately hand it over to the recruitment department, which worked on finding the candidates. Once that task was done, the account executive/client relations department would take over. All of this happened with very limited communication between departments, unless there was some success and we all celebrated a bit.

I did all of this because I didn't want anyone in the company to learn too many trade secrets. So by keeping everyone separated, the sales people did not know the candidates, the recruiters did not know the clients, and everyone worked on a need-to-know basis. I might have had more protection from my employees stealing candidates and ideas, but people were far less invested in the success of the entire process as a result of my paranoia. Changing my approach and deciding to let everyone participate in the entire cycle from A to Z created a much stronger team, with people independently generating new ideas. Unless your business exists in a niche that comes with heavy security needs, you should be putting most of your resources into transparency and empowerment instead.

That said, you do need to devote at least some attention to protecting client data, and you still need to hold the employees that have access to that data to a higher standard. So when it comes to my account executives and accountant, I still make them sign a heavy duty contract that's intimidating and makes clear that I can afford the lawyers that they cannot. As counterproductive as it can be, I do need to work once in a while with clients who need that extra protection from the candidate that they hire. It could be because that person is dealing with privileged information or products with real security concerns. The way I solve the problem for them is that I find the most reputable law firm in the region of the candidate, and invite the person to that firm. They sign the document, and get their picture taken while signing it. If the candidate for some reason thinks of any malpractice, he sees that our client means business, and has access to the kind of powerful lawyers he'll have to go against if he gets caught.

Again if I haven't made it clear, I'm extremely against this practice 99% of the time. A candidate *usually* should not be introduced to a company through intimidation, since that's hurting morale even before they get to judge if their new boss is a jerk. But if it's absolutely necessary, this will scare the crap out of 99% of any remote or offshore people who are considering doing something unethical. And by the way, for all the people who assume that when you go to a corrupt country you don't have protection. I have a small secret to tell you: The top law firms in some of those countries are elite, because they know how to maneuver through this kind of corruption. What I'm saying is that when someone lives far away in a country where you don't really know how things function, the idea that you suddenly lose all legal protection is simply false.

Still, the biggest concern that a security-intensive company should be worried about when they hire a remote employee is not whether there's going to be malpractice; it's whether there might be a security infringement. In other words, the biggest emphasis is not to protect a company from the employees, but to protect employees from themselves. This is where we get to the most important part of this section, because security issues based on technology are the biggest concern. This is one of the biggest reasons that banks, government offices, and other high-security companies often avoid using remote employees. That status quo might change a bit given the impact of COVID-19, considering that eventually these organizations will have to send someone home, and they need to figure out how to do that safely.

So how do we deal with security? How do we make sure that even with the most caring employee will not have security breaches? Here are the tips that I offer my clients when needed:

Ship a fully encrypted company laptop

If you buy a laptop (or desktop) for your local employee, it's not going to cost much more than buying and shipping one to your remote employee. The laptop will have similar configurations to your office network, with strict security procedures. I was weighing whether to explain in this book how to do this, but honestly if you are not an IT guy you probably should let a professional do it, because while it is not so difficult to encrypt a laptop, performing the next step is.

Set Up a VPN

VPN stands for virtual private network. A long time ago, in order to make a company secure, you just needed a building, some locks, and a few security guards to keep the weirdos out. The introduction of the Internet created a new, highly vulnerable weak point, one that required a whole new set of security procedures. In the 90s and early 2000s, people started accessing their office computers from remote locations with applications like GoToMyPC and LogMeIn. That brought new security challenges, because it extended your network to the virtual world. So suddenly a computer in another state or even another country has become part of your network, and needs to follow the same security procedures as your internal network. So setting up a secure virtual network became key to protecting your data.

Now it's important to mention that you can encrypt the laptop yourself and you can set up your own VPN. But real security is not something that you solve in one day — it's something that you have to constantly monitor. Which means the more security-intensive your company is, the more specialized the IT and security departments have to be. It is highly recommended to have a dedicated IT person or team that's not overburdened with work. The reason why the calm schedule is so important is because you want the team (or company) to get highly familiar with your network and can take the time to understand it perfectly They also need to be available to address security threats at a moment's notice. That said, with proper encryption, proper updating of your network, and a VPN, you can eliminate most security concerns.

Password Management

If your boss keeps using his wife's favorite shampoo as the password for every login, it could eventually lead to disaster...and no, changing every o to a zero won't help. In an office environment, you need everyone to be more responsible with their passwords. After trying all the password managers available on the market, 1Password is the one that we enjoyed using the most;

after extensive research, we found that it was one of the only password management apps that hadn't been hacked or leaked. It's a Canadian company that has all the right features that allow you to restrict or grant access as needed. It also works on most platforms and mobile solutions, so that you truly have a centralized password solution. This way even if someone steals your computer, they will never gain access to your info, and that's good policy for any company.

Wiping and location software

If a thief does get his hands on your laptop, the passwords are not the only thing you should be worried about — it's your data in general. That's why you need an app that wipes your data when emergencies happen. I have been looking for Mission Impossible-type self-destruct software, but since that doesn't exist yet in real life, a wiping app will have to do for now.

The good news is that there are many great apps you can install on your laptop or phone that do just that. One of the most popular apps to wipe and encrypt your database is DriveStrike. It is an affordable app that can be used for individuals or for widespread, company-wide data destruction. What gives DriveStrike software an edge and makes it the favorite of large corporations is that it not only wipes data from devices when necessary. It also encrypts, locks, and locates your hardware. Just imagine the ability to

trace and catch a thief. That would be so much fun...
or potentially suicidal. On second thought, maybe
you should just call the police.

Enable two-factor authentication or use an authentication app

I consider secure authentication a must, since having
to confirm a person's identity can reduce the risks of
hackers or intruders accessing your data and sensitive
information. A hacker would then need to generate
a one-time code that expires after a certain period
of time, your authenticator app, and your security
key — which is virtually impossible. While the
hacker is trying to access all that information, you're
alerted that someone is trying to access a personal or
business account to steal or copy information. That
way you can help the person take action by changing
passwords, backing up information, and protecting
data before anything bad happens.

I do have to remind the real security-intensive
companies that your security will only be as good as
the focus of your IT specialist. So again: you need to
make sure that you have a dedicated, highly paid IT
specialist who is focused at all times on securing the
virtual network and the computers belonging to your
remote team.

For companies with a lower budget and less urgent
security needs, try to get your employees to install

all the tools we've discussed on their laptops. Also, if possible, ask them to dedicate their laptops mostly to work.

I hope you and your remote business now feel a lot more secure.

VI - HEALTH AND COMPANY
CULTURE

Managing Mental Health

I have a confession to make: For years I have been
jealous of several startup companies that generate
probably a quarter of the revenue that my company
does. That's because when you walk into those places,
you see a bunch of people shooting Nerf guns,
hanging out, and having cool happy hours. When I
got into business, I never imagined I would be sitting
in front of a computer by myself at home, tapping
away all day. As an extrovert I legitimately felt lonely,
and I had to put in extra effort to get out and socialize,
which thank G-d was something I was good at. I'm
also glad that at least doing sales for DistantJob was a
very social experience and required me to go to many
conferences.

This has slowly changed as I started creating a company culture and forging deep relationships with my employees. When the conferencing tools started functioning well and webcam conversations became standard, things definitely got better. We even started having drinks and small social parties. It's not perfect (I still can't shoot anyone with a Nerf gun), but it certainly became a more social environment.

It's funny that I have a closed office in a co-working space one block from my house, where most of the other individuals are from small startups or other companies, and all they hear is this crazy person celebrating, laughing, being rowdy and sometimes even shouting to his computer. I'm without a doubt the coworking space's crazy guy.

Unfortunately not everyone is as lucky. There is no question that working in front of a computer all day can be lonely. As far as I'm concerned this is one of the biggest obstacles for remote work, including as a manager. Yes, remote workers have been shown to be happier than your standard employee. But if you don't stay vigilant, the isolation that comes with remote work can lead to depression and other mental health issues. If that happens, the best-case scenario is that you'll lose an employee. Yes I said best-case scenario, because an even worse situation is having someone sitting there getting paid and not really producing. When it comes to mental health I'm not saying that the bottom line is the most important concern — caring for people should be. But for some people, you need to hit them in the pocket. So here it is: Caring = Money.

So let's talk about some research. According to the Buffer State of Remote Work Survey, 22% of remote workers can't unplug after work, and more importantly 19% feel lonely[7]. Remote work can come with extremes; tons of people are happier when they work from home, but if socially neglected there is also a lot more chance for them to feel worse off than when they worked in the office.

It's simply a reality that in the office, because people hang out and work with each other, they also check in on one another. Both managers and colleagues can see who is doing well and who is not. They can see if someone is getting burned out. These are luxuries that remote people do not have. The management of your employees' mental health is probably the biggest difference between a local environment and a remote one. That's why there needs to be a much bigger emphasis on getting to know your people. This can include getting to know their hobbies, their kids, and their personalities. Group meetings should always have a social aspect. Spend part of your Monday meeting learning what the team did during the weekend, socially. Sometimes that can be more beneficial for your company than discussing work.

---

7   https://buffer.com/state-of-remote-work-2019

We spent a full chapter discussing how to build trust with your employees without consequences, but we didn't discuss how this trust should expand to mental health. Make it clear to them that if they feel burned out, harassed, hurt, or depressed, they can tell you about it. Get to know your people on a personal basis, connect with them, learn their children's names and their favorite hobbies. I do judge my managers by whether or not they know about their workers' pets. If you create a strong company culture, you can almost have the same check-in experience that you have in the office.

What Is Culture?

Ahhhhh *culture*, my favorite buzzword. Just saying that word makes me happy. Who wouldn't want to have an amazing company culture? When I think about culture, I imagine the lifestyle at Google or Facebook, where employees lounge around, play ping pong, and have the most incredible happy hours, yet somehow everybody is incredibly productive.

I don't know anyone under the age of 40 who runs a business and does not want to have an amazing work culture. But in practice, culture can be a bit of a money drain. Even worse, many people don't really understand what culture is.

When I offer consulting for clients, I always discuss the need to replicate the most effective processes and cultural elements in your company. On a broad level, the process is fairly easy to define: It's the way you train. It's the way you motivate. It's the way you qualify. It's the way you interview. But building a great company culture tends to be a lot more complicated to define. For many people, culture is just an unclear word that people enjoy using, like "holistic," "cloud," and "supercalifragilisticexpialidocious"...and yes I'm feeling supercalifragilisticexpialidocious right now. When I first tried to learn about implementing culture in my company, I did a lot of research and found that even the people who were providing the definitions were not 100% clear about the answer. I just saw buzzwords defining other buzzwords.

Some people would say that culture is a company's personality. Or another favorite, it is the DNA of the company. Other places were giving the most complicated definitions. I looked at Wikipedia, and they defined cultures as values and behaviors that contribute to the unique social and psychological environment of a business. Investopedia says that corporate culture refers to the beliefs and behaviors that determine how a company's employees and management interact and handle outside business transactions. Now that is a mouthful.

So I realized that I need to come up with a clearer definition to suit my company's needs and goals. Now, just a disclaimer for any sticklers out there. The definition of culture that I use, which I'm about to share, might not be the exact dictionary definition. It might not cover everything that culture has to offer. But it is without a doubt the most actionable definition that I can offer. So what is culture in a company? *For me, it means connection.*

I know. I know. Again, it's a buzzword defining a buzzword. So let's get into this some more. When you make a choice to invest in your company culture, what you're really doing is investing in activities, processes, and strategies that get your people more connected to their company, and more connected to other people in the company. As a bonus, they also become more connected to the clients.

Now let's dive even deeper. When we get people to connect to our company, one of our first reflexes is to create benefits and social activities that make people feel happy to be there. But to be clear, happiness is not the only way to get people to feel more attached to the company.

Let's take Steve Jobs as an example. Jobs was far from a specialist when it came to employee happiness, and that is an understatement. He would make people work 12 hours a day, and his incredibly high standards for his employees often created a stressful environment.

Yet *he gave them a challenge.* He gave them a feeling that they were creating incredible value. Everybody who is using any Apple product today feels that the technology they are holding in their hands is incredibly innovative, and Jobs' team made that happen. He specialized in creating passion and getting his people excited about innovation. This made his people feel a belonging to the company, and to the Apple brand. In order to get people connected to the company, you need to focus on comfort and happiness...and also passion.

Still, when it comes to getting your employees to feel connected to the company they work for, employee-to-employee connections are equally important, if not more. While there are still quite a few companies that care more about individual productivity, in most modern businesses teamwork is an essential component for success. That means when you focus on teamwork, you want to get people to feel as actively connected to each other as possible.

When people think about creating culture, they often think in terms of social activities such as happy hours, barbecues, and group outings for team bonding. There is also the water cooler hangout, and favorite lunch places to chat with our colleagues. We try to hire people who are on the same wavelength as the rest of the team.

The reason why we do all of this is to get people to connect with each other with the expected benefit of creating exceptional teams. That's why you're investing in culture. You're really investing in getting people to work better with each other.

Last but not least is the connection to your clients. This of course isn't relevant to everybody in your company — just the people who talk to the clients. Yet overall company culture does very much affect our interaction with clients. For instance, if your target market consists of people in fashion, your employees should know the best places to purchase a Louis Vuitton handbag or Gucci boots. I actually don't know if Gucci makes boots, but somehow I hear all about them in movies. If your target market is sports and athletes, you should have people in your company who at least watch some football, soccer, and basketball. If you infect people with passion for their company, it will transmit to the clients. At DistantJob, we are incredibly passionate about remote work, and our salespeople and customer service infect our clients with the same passion. (Isn't it nice to discuss infecting people in a positive way?)

Now, why am I discussing culture so much in a remote work book? Even more importantly, why am I discussing connection?

Well, it's because culture is all about connection, and remote employees tend to be the most disconnected people in your company, so if your company is completely remote, there's an even bigger challenge when it comes to connection. That's why culture has to become an even greater point of emphasis if you are moving to a remote working environment.

TAKEAWAY:

Culture is about connection, how people feel a sense of belonging to the company, as well as teamwork and understanding of clients.

Define your company culture

Understanding what culture means and defining connection already gets you halfway to actually creating the amazing culture you want. That said, while it's a good idea to define your culture, like a birth plan it rarely ends up going exactly how you expect.

When I started DistantJob, for me it was about passion for remote. I remember hiring a sales guy with lots of promise who started annoying me in his second week of the job. When I asked how he liked the service that he was selling, he answered that it's really all about the money for him. He didn't even humor me. So the second I saw that he was not producing, I was sooo glad to show him the door. It's too bad I missed this guy's lack of passion when I interviewed him. I really want people who are passionate about remote work; if you're not, honesty is overrated in this circumstance.

As the company grew, our team's culture began to emerge, as we oriented ourselves into increasingly frequent nerdy discussions. We expanded to discuss music, fantasy books/comics, food, and even politics, all of it done with great humor. I particularly enjoyed our food discussions, because I got to explore food from all over the world. The political discussions do sometimes make me concerned that we might hurt someone's feelings, but we try hard to hire pretty chill people who can keep an open mind.

In the 100th episode of the DistantJob Podcast, my director of marketing Luis asked me how he, our VP of Operations Rustam, and I got so close. My answer was that there simply isn't any limit to what we can discuss. The ability to hang with someone and have time pass without even noticing is a sign of people who are truly connected. That's why when you recruit someone, part of the interview process should be to have the applicant hang out with a few members of the team. This way, we can naturally see if the potential candidate fits with the team, without going through strict definitions of our company culture.

I also work hard to get my team to understand technology and get them excited about remote management. We connect people to the company by paying attention to the wellbeing of employees and preaching about the remote revolution that anyone can be passionate about. We connect the team to one another with endless conversations about nerdy and funny topics. We connect with our clients by becoming experts in technology and remove management. We define our entire culture with the goal to connect.

Activities to improve connection and culture

One of the biggest challenges of creating a virtual culture is that people are not actually there. I take pride in finding new strategies to connect and become friends (not just colleagues) with my employees. Here's a list of things we do to foster that kind of relationship, combined with some other unusual but fun ideas.

Get Personal in Meetings

Meetings offer a rare opportunity to get your distributed team together at the same time, so make the most of it. Don't just think of it as an occasion to talk business and get through the agenda; it's also valuable team bonding time. Set aside some time at the beginning of the meeting to chat, just as you would if you were sitting in a meeting room waiting for everyone to turn up. As the group leader, you can help the conversation flow, and give your team something to talk about. This is also an excellent opportunity to mention any birthdays or personal milestones and celebrate them together.

Sharing hobbies

We share a lot of hobbies. In our company Slack channel, we have a few categories for foodies, music, pets, and video games. We have a true virtual water cooler, where we love to share and to talk. I totally give my VP credit for getting that exciting environment rolling, but by it's taken on a life of its own.

Having drinks and celebrating birthdays

Who said you need a bar to hang out for a drink? Every month or so, we take a few hours to sit down and have a drink. The rules are that you don't have to drink alcohol, but you must bring some kind of drink, such as coffee or tea as an alternative. In other words we don't encourage alcoholism, just hydration. Well, hydration with caffeine. OK, so just a fun hangout.

Most of the time these get-togethers are to celebrate the birthdays of that month, or some special achievement. It's a great experience just to stay social and get to know the group in a relaxed environment.

One-on-one meetings

Slack has this incredible feature called Donut, which randomly picks two members of a team for a one-on-one hangout. It's a great way to get to know people on a more intimate basis. After each meeting, these two people share on Basecamp what they learned about each other.

Playing board games and card games virtually

Just to be clear, this is different from playing video games together. The idea is to play online games that force you to socialize and interact with one another, where you still can see each other on Zoom while you play these games. We just discovered Cards Against Humanity's virtual version and absolutely love it. Some of us also play Settlers of Catan and Warhammer 40,000: Space Marine.

Virtual Scavenger Hunts

Divide employees into teams and give each team an identical list of items to "find." This will ideally be things in their cities such as playgrounds, fountains, or a city limits sign. Assign a team captain who will delegate certain finds to each person.

The team captain will collect photographs of the finds and then post them to a board or job in your task management system. The first team to locate all the items wins.

Host a contest or game

Contests are a great way to spur productivity and help employees motivate each other. They do not always have to involve work-related activities. Contests that encourage people to work out more, eat healthier, or learn a new skill can all be great ways to build and encourage teamwork.

When holding a contest, set clear rules and deadlines so that everyone knows what to expect ahead of time. Just be sure to make the contest fair and appealing to a wide group of people. Don't forget to post results so that each person has a chance to congratulate the winner.

Become your team's therapist

At DistantJob, our mission is to create independent, empowered managers and employees.

I've learned the importance of empowering your team and their independence. To give them the opportunity to fail, and learn from their mistakes. The goal is that with that kind of guidance, your team members will become more talented than you are in their specific skills. In my company I felt that I'd succeeded in creating a great culture when I transformed from the idea creator, mentor, and motivator to the company plumber, therapist, and entertainer.

Yes you heard me right...I'm a plumber. A huge part of my job is to continuously plug leaks in company productivity. I need to analyze the pipes of the company and fix them. Any weakness the company has, I need to work with team members to address the issue. In any growing company, nothing ever grows perfectly smoothly. When my business development department is doing well, suddenly the bottleneck becomes operations. Then I need to bring recruitment up to par. Suddenly, recruitment is doing such a good job that you need to swing the focus back to BizDev. It never ends, which is what we call a good problem to have. If you're really succeeding, you can even delegate another team member to take over some of the plumbing work.

Even more important than the plumbing work is my role as company therapist. This is all about

making sure that my teams are all functioning well. While I don't have any degrees in psychology, it does feel like I am generating a lot of experience as a therapist. Even in a company with a team working in total unison, there will always be a member of the team who develops some kind of frustration and resentment.

That frustration and resentment could be with another team member. Or maybe it's a salary issue. Or it could be someone getting fed up with being stuck in the same position. Even if you push hard for open communications, there might be someone who doesn't share what's frustrating him. The more that issue is ignored, the more that team member will become distant and untrusting.

This is an issue that happens a lot more in remote environments, because people are not in each other's face every day the way they are in a physical office, so they do not need to confront each other. They can just disappear to Angryland. So it's all up to you, Mr. Manager. Pay attention to early signs, as they usually come in as passive-aggressive messages. If you create enough trust in the beginning, those messages will become more assertive and productive rather than passive, aggressive, or passive-aggressive.

Confront the problem as soon you see that something is wrong, because if you do it too late, that team member might just leave before you know it. If the issue is a conflict with another team member, you must ensure that it's a constructive conflict. Sometimes the so-called constructive conflict is not so constructive and might end up becoming hurtful instead. The debates that you introduce could potentially be what ignites the anger in the first place, and that's OK. Constructive conflicts are an absolute necessity in a healthy working environment and amazing managers don't back off from their expectations — they learn how to ease people into them. They treat their colleagues with respect and explain to them why working through problems honestly and openly is important.

It's important because that's how you get real challenges and not just fake approvals. When people are angry, listen to them, hear their pain but make it clear that what you are doing is not making life difficult for them, but rather investing in them. The ability to handle real, challenging conversation makes them better — better workers and better leaders. If it's an issue between two colleagues, bring them back to the conversation and moderate, but don't stop until the relationship comes back to mutual respect again, or at least mutual acceptance. One key to think about when you moderate or discuss frustrations is that you are not searching for who is right; you are figuring out how to work together in a comfortable and productive working environment.

Of course there are times when a person has changed and does not fit your company's culture anymore, then you might need to let him go. But when you start with a new employee, it's an investment by itself that consumes time, resources and money. So you might want to double down on making your existing people better.

TAKEAWAY:

Pay attention to early signs of frustration, and create and encourage constructive conflict.

VII - THE FIRST FEW WEEKS

Onboarding

Most successful companies have mastered their onboarding processes. The habits that successful companies instill in their employees during their first few weeks on the job will guide them through the rest of their careers. I can't start breaking down the onboarding process of each company, but what I can offer you is the add-on piece for remote employees. Solid onboarding is required for any new employees, but it's especially important for remote workers because there are many concepts that are still so foreign, to them and maybe even to you. Even people that have done some kind of remote work for many years could have been completely mismanaged, considering that the study of remote management is still young.

Whether people have just transferred home from their office or have been working remotely most of their professional lives, they will have tons of misconceptions about what it means to be a real remote employee.

In earlier chapters I discussed *not* calling people outsourcers or freelancers. Thinking they still get to function like a freelancer is a big part of the misconception that I get with new recruits. People still come in with a non-committal mentality, hoping to create a lifestyle job with unlimited flexibility. Increased flexibility and a more rewarding lifestyle are not bad things in themselves, of course. But some individuals take on a more individualistic approach and see work as simply separate projects that they must complete in order to get paid. As a boss or manager you don't want that kind of transactional relationship. What you really want is someone who is invested in the success of the team and long-term strategy of the company, not just the project in front of a person's nose at this very minute.

You need to make it clear that this is not contract work. It's not freelancing. It's a real job, just like what would be expected from you in the office. So yes, remote employees are expected to work eight hours a day. Yes they're supposed to have some kind of schedule. If the company is flexible, great, they still need to have some kind of concept where they work and maintain an easy communication process. Most importantly, an employee needs to be integrated into the processes and culture of the company, and be a contributing member of the team. That means an employee has a responsibility not only to succeed in a specific task but also to help the rest of the team succeed, because that's really what matters.

As a manager, you must use your intuition when employees start acting too much like freelancers, and bring them back to employee reality. If your Spidey sense is not fully functioning to figure this out, just ask the person about how the group is progressing. If the answer devolves into discussion about personal achievements, that's not good. Also a problem is the consultant mentality that strictly focuses on group achievements, when it's not clear what the individual has achieved by herself. So keep your eyes on both type of mentalities. To build an amazing team, you need people who see the success of the company and their own as being always connected.

That's why the onboarding is so crucial: because all of these goals need to be spelled out and clarified during the training. With people who come from the remote world, you will need to be a stickler. It's important to lay out your company's ground rules and your remote worker-specific mindset during their first week on the job, before bad habits start to build. But for the love of everything holy, please don't point to someone and say, "You look like a freelancer, shape up!" Define the mindset in positive terms, and clarify the importance and vision of the team as a whole.

Make sure to set your expectations clearly. If an employee is not busy in the office, make it clear he shouldn't expect people to chase after him, nor start working like a chicken with its head cut off just to keep himself busy. Set your expectations, your methods of communications, and your specific outreach methods for each person and each specific situation. In my office I try to make myself available, and I make it clear that I'm not impressed with people who are "afraid to bother me." Actually that is one of the most annoying comments that I get when someone completely goes in the wrong direction: "I was afraid to bother you." For crying out loud, don't be afraid to bother me or message me. If I'm busy, I'm perfectly capable of putting my phone on silent and responding to your Slack message later.

Also, whatever you do, don't disappear. It's already challenging enough to follow up with remote employees. If you are sick and can't work, let your boss know. I don't care if you are in the hospital, with today's technology it's easy to send an email or a message to make it clear that you won't be available, or worst-case scenario get your partner or parents to message us.

(Venting done.)

I like to think I'm a happy, easygoing boss, but nothing annoys me more than unexplained disappearances, and I try to make that clear from day one. That's the type of expectation you should be setting that first week.

Speaking of parents and partners, when you start with a new employee, gather all emergency contact info. Just recently we got the unfortunate news that one of the candidates we'd provided to a client had died from complications related to COVID-19. I do have to say, nothing hits home that this disease is real and dangerous like when it hits someone you know. This was an incredibly tragic situation, and I'm so glad we were able to contact this person's sister and help her any way we could. Considering that this person lived on the other side of the world, his family and friends had no clue what he was working on and for who. When people from this mysterious North American company reached out, the family was so appreciative to get to know some of his colleagues, and were deeply touched by the help of that company and DistantJob, simply because we took down all the right contact info.

Another good step to take is to define how you want to learn about daily tasks and projects. Some managers like to talk on the phone every day. Some like to visit with or be visited by each employee. Some prefer to just get updates from their senior people. At DistantJob we tend to have a sprint meeting at the beginning of the week and then daily updates of tasks on Basecamp. I always define the software and apps that my company uses and how we use them, and you should do the same. That goes for everything from Slack to Zoom to Grammarly, and of course project management software, which needs extra attention considering that every company utilizes that kind of software differently.

You absolutely need to define values. For example, at DistantJob we are a mistake-friendly environment, so we expect you to take more risk. We really like contributions, and as a boss I'm perfectly happy to be challenged. We are really not impressed with people holding back.

So here's what you need to think about:

- Discuss if you are comfortable with flexible hours or if you want staff to work strict shift hours. At DistantJob we try to keep things flexible for most roles, but like to have approximate working hours and communication time.

- Discuss how much time is dedicated to creative work and structured work; some companies, like Google, give a day to create new things.

- Discuss your expectations regarding social gatherings. Do you have to come? Are these gatherings encouraged, or are they truly optional? At DistantJob, they are heavily encouraged.

The key to all this is that you can't be wishy-washy. You must define your processes, values, and expectations clearly, because in the remote world, people often drift toward their own ways of doing things if they don't have proper guidance.

And again, if you hired a person who has freelanced for a long time, you have to scare that freelancer mentality out of him. Sorry, I know that sounds a bit rude. But as a boss we often try to invest in processes. The moment someone joins your company, physically or virtually, he became part of something bigger than himself.

TAKEAWAYS:

Eliminate non-committal mentality from day one and make sure that workers invest in the success of the team and long-term vision of the company.

Agree on approximate hours, communication expectations, and how to report tasks.

Make it clear that disappearance sucks and take down emergency contact info.

Define your Expectations for Onboarding

A question that came up often when I first started DistantJob was whether remote worker candidates could be asked to do jobs that are standard in a regular office environment. Another question we got was: "Can we expect the person to finish the work at this time?" I found those questions really weird.

I realize that when I started the company I was focused only on cost from offshore regions. Back then I didn't fully understand the benefits of not being limited to one area. So the focus was really on value...and I'm only using the word value because my marketing teacher always taught me that I shouldn't use the word cheap, because back then the offshore world was soooooo cheap. Offshore programmers worked for about 10% of the cost of local salaries. This made some employers feel a little uncomfortable about asking certain things from remote workers that would be completely expected from local employees.

In fact, not only should you have the same expectations for remote workers as you do for local employees...you could even expect more, considering all the benefits of remote work. The key message here is that you must treat any foreign employee as if she's getting a premium North American salary. If you treat someone like a cheap employee not only are you not going to get the same level of production...you'll get less. For all who are having a hard time setting up expectations for your remote people here's how you would do it

Take a few hours with your top managers and start writing down your processes. Note down what you and your managers do during the day or during a week. What keeps you busy. Break down the actions of the day that involve producing and managing your people. What do you ask your people to do?

What are you lenient about, and where is there no compromise? For coders it's the way they comment in your codebase, for salespeople it's the formula to turn a lead into a client.

Analyzing your day will help you define your procedures and methodologies and most importantly what you expect out of your people. It might also help you define what doesn't work with your processes. We talk in the book a lot about distractions and bad meetings, and this might be the time for strategy changes, or at least trying get a bit leaner with things that you most certainly don't need to replicate in a remote environment.

If you are starting from scratch and don't have a team yet, now is a perfect time to study a management methodology. Figure out the type of person you are. Are you detail-oriented? Do you like to plan in advance or simply go with the flow? Do you want to start learning about Agile, waterfall, and subsets such as Kanban and Scrum...or even get certified in PMP? Then finally, define your culture (as discussed in detail in the previous chapter). Once you have written all that down, you clearly understand the expectation from your people and for that matter your future remote people. If you are taking remote work seriously you should spend at least 10-20 hours with your team to do this right. If you are just hiring one person, then two hours would suffice. Just keep in mind that defining your processes and company culture are important exercises. To understand this topic in more depth I recommend reading a book called *Traction* by Gino Wickman.

So what's next? Think about the best way to replicate your expectations of a local worker in a remote environment, and the challenges you might face in doing so. For some people it will come naturally. You might just be the "I talk to each of my employees once a day and I don't see any reason why I can't just do the same on video" guy. For others it might be more complicated. You might be the "I like to sit with my entire team around the table, have some beers and get some creative juices flowing" guy. We already covered how you might be able to get almost the same experience through technology. Now all you need to do is ship your teammates some specialty artisanal microbrews and you might not miss the old ways at all. Once you get your expectations defined, interviewing prospective remote workers should be a breeze, or at least no different than interviewing local ones. If you suck at interviewing, you might need to read a few more books after this.

Don't settle for anyone you don't understand, or anyone who can't understand what you're saying. Language is key and a major source of frustration when it comes out blurry. In the long run even if the candidate is very talented, he will eventually make costly mistakes because of the communication challenge.

So don't be afraid to set your expectations higher. The world is big and you can get a little pickier with what you want and need.

TAKEAWAY:

Set your expectations even higher than local employees and treat them like any local employee you would have.

Treat your foreign employees as if they are getting North American salaries. This will change the way you see them.

VIII – FINAL POINTERS

Advice for the Adviceless

"Alright Sharon, cut the crap. I run a $2 billion company that's growing exponentially every year. I'm tough, I'm aggressive but I have my people's respect and for all I care this is how I define my culture. I honestly don't need advice from the head of a 30-employee company about my processes. Talk to me when you reach half of what I have reached, OK? I like the old-school approach of supervising and micromanaging my managers for 10 hours a day, and I teach them to supervise and micromanage their own employees the same way. I don't want to change. This model has been good for me, and I have no interest in fixing what is already working. The only reason why I'm talking to a chump like you is because I have been forced into this hellhole called remote because of this stupid virus, and I could use a few tips."

My response:

Alright Mr. Multi-Billionaire Fancy Pants, I get it. You don't need improvement in processes, you have a successful model. You just need help with the transition to remote during the pandemic. The truth is that you are kind of right. Different kinds of companies have different winning strategies that don't necessarily need changing. These processes are the soul of the business and these processes are truly what makes it work. Going remote is a great opportunity to change, but maybe you are a dynamic company that continuously changes and improves already. Maybe you are a company with a unique product or service, so what I'm suggesting is not relevant to you at all. In that case, here are a few key suggestions on remote management for someone who's already figured out everything else about running a business:

1. Buy each of your employees a quality headset and proper webcam, while upgrading their Internet and routers. That goes double for CEOs who rule with such an iron first that every time you ask your employees to jump, they ask how high. You really want to make sure that the audio does not skip on you at the exact moment when you ask them to jump. That would be awkward.

2. If you are keen to replicate your office experience, make sure that when you talk to

people, you are on a webcam a lot. You simply do not get the same interaction through audio communication only. So that means that if in the past you randomly appeared at an employee's desk, asked him questions, and then dealt with his mistake, in a remote environment you need to send a Zoom link and follow the same procedure. If you want to deliver a message to your entire office in the conference room, bring them all to Zoom and deliver that message.

3. Set your expectations clearly in the first week. Some of your employees might have certain misconceptions because they are working remotely. Set your rules, let them know whether you want them to work a set regular shift or if you are comfortable with some flexibility. If you are not flexible, use the same set of rules you would use in the office. For instance, the "I was in the toilet" excuse can only be used twice without repercussions. Make it clear to your employees that you will be working on intuition and if many things sound like excuses you will assume exactly that. If you are running a tough environment you should be clear about it. Again this is not my way of doing things, but I also don't run a $2 billion business.

4. In onboarding, define your communication expectations. While I like to keep a chill working environment, even I get annoyed when someone is waiting for me to tell them what to do while twiddling their thumbs or working randomly just to make themselves look busy. Even worse, I can't stand people who just suddenly disappear. Unfortunately, some people have misconceptions about the liberties they can take when working remotely. So you must clearly define your company's ground rules for all workers, whether they're in the office or remote.

5. Check their mental health. I know, I know, a tough boss like you does not care about your employees' mental health. If they can't cope, they should find themselves another job, right? Wrong!!!!! First, boo to you. Besides, you need to understand that the importance of employee mental health becomes magnified in the remote world. This transition could be very challenging, especially for the old-school managers who work under you. If you are not going to pay attention to them, you might lose a lot of people, or even worse, you might end up keeping unproductive people on payroll. You need to offer a more personal touch in the remote environment. Sorry, but that's the deal.

Structure, routine and focus in a flexible environment

One of the most popular concepts used in the remote community is the idea of asynchronous vs. synchronous.

If the terms are not clear, the idea of synchronous involves working in real time. It is having all people work at the same time and responding to each other immediately. It is mimicking the office experience. An asynchronous environment on the other hand is when you send a message and let people respond when they can. Of course these terms are mostly related to text/chat messages, although I have noticed lately that more and more people leave voice messages in chat-based programs. The reason why people are very careful with synchronous communication or replicating the office experience too much is because of fear of distraction. In an asynchronous environment, people simply respond to you when they are free.

So here's the deal. Distraction concerns are very real, but too many people preach completely flexible, asynchronous work and that comes with its own consequences. I feel a bit like the old man in the remote community, because when you hear *flexible,* I hear *non-committal.* Yes it is the non-committal thing again. I hope I'm not going to have an army of consultants and freelancers chasing me after this, but choosing to focus on strictly full-time people with somewhat less flexibility is where I really differentiate from the crowd.

Don't get me wrong, I do believe in some *healthy* flexibility. Giving people specific eight-hour shifts that can never change might be too rigid. If a person is truly not productive on a given day, for any reason (whether, they are sick, distracted, or had too much to drink the day before), tell them to take the day off, go do something else, and come back when they're ready to do focused work. That said, I do like to understand the general core hours of my team. I want to know when I can expect to reach them. While I'm very conscious about distractions when I need to reach you, I do want you to be available during those approximate working hours.

I specifically remember the time a member of my marketing team did not show up for the end-of-year group event. When I asked her manager why she was the only one who did not show up, he said because she did not wake up — and the hangout happened during her core hours. I remember being particularly annoyed with that answer, because I want my people to be honest with me...but sometimes coming up with an excuse at least shows that you care. I know I'm being a bit contradictory, but I want my people to have responsibility, and if they drop the ball, to offer a proper apology or at least give me a reasonable excuse. Bonus points if it's a ridiculous excuse, like a tiger ate my iPhone or I was abducted by incredibly amusing aliens who forced me to have a few drinks with them.

Every noise maker in the remote world keeps sitting down and discussing how things change and how you must accept the change because nothing will be the same. But don't worry, you can get used to it. I accept that there is a lot of room for improvement if you need the improvement. I also truly believe that if you've done your job well as a manager in a physical office, if you motivated and trained your people, inspired them, created relationships, and managed distractions well, not much will change in the remote world. My job is simply to inform you of what you can't get away with in the remote world that might have passed for acceptable in the office world.

I truly believe that a team is only as good as the manager, and that a manager's job is to invest in structure. Imposing daily routines helps people become more effective, reduce bad habits, create fewer daily blocks, and reduce stress. You can call me an old fogey, see if I care.

Structure starts with people coming on time to work. Yes, I know it sounds funny when I talk about coming to work on time when all you're doing is going from your bed to your desk at home. Still, as an employee, you have to show the discipline to arrive at that desk at a specific time, then having your chat status turned to available for the rest of the day. If you're busy that chat status can say busy...just never away. If you follow the Agile path of defining your daily tasks, defining those tasks at a specific time announces to the world that you are around. The remote world provides the opportunity to find the best time and environment to be more productive, and that is truly awesome.

Just as signaling the start of your day is important, defining the end of your work day at a specific time is also useful. As a manager you need to negotiate (not dictate) those hours and tasks and make sure your remote employees stick to them.

And with that, I now sound like a tyrant in the remote community.

The reality is that you can't implement structure and routine unless you deal with someone who is really a focused full-time employee. That's why I invest so much in the discussion of non-committal workers such as consultants and freelancers. I'm not saying that you can't produce quality work when you work on or think about more than one project. But it is incredibly challenging to learn the processes and routines of a company while investing in the success of the team when you're constantly multi-tasking, or your mind is on something other than the task that's right in front of you.

And forget about integrating into the culture when you have remote workers who are all over the place....

it's not happening. If you want to get the most out of your worker, make sure that you're investing in their focus. Make sure that the person feels like she is part of the culture, that her opinions matter, that her mental health matters, that she is not separated from the clique, and that she gets similar benefits compared to local employees. Most importantly make it clear that this is a real, full-time, permanent job, even if some remote workers might officially be classified as contractors. I know this doesn't make me very popular with all marketplaces and contractor-for-hire services, but I have gained the most out of my employees when I get the opportunity to invest in them first.

Yes, the office can be distracting, the process could be overdue for change, and the culture could be dry. But there is still a potential reality that you might be underestimating your company, and that you may just need to replicate existing processes for the remote work environment. Remote work does give you a bit more room for flexibility, and I do believe in taking advantage of it; but completely asynchronous work does take away from the company experience. Unless the time zones do not allow it, I really do believe that a company should have at least four hours of crossover, approximate shifts, and defined communication tools.

TAKEAWAY:

Whether you are more or less flexible, it's good to agree on some kind of schedule with a beginning and an end, and use those opportunities to define your daily tasks and results.

Always remove the misconception that remote means do what you want when you want in a noncommittal style. Invest in your employees' focus and structure.

Part II - Advice for Remote Workers

I - A NEW WORLD

Many new remote employees have just sat down in front of their laptop at home and realized that this might be *the reality* for the next month...or maybe the next two years.

For many of you, the concept of working at home is absolutely exciting. No more daily commute in traffic, no more late nights without seeing your kids. You can eat your own food, even stay in your pajamas. Yet for some of us, it is a scary concept. A new environment, a new way of working, it all just sounds scary.

I'm here for you guys. Let me offer you a guide on how to do this right. With this guide, you won't just get comfortable with the new working arrangement. You'll get your boss to start rethinking why he didn't notice you for that promotion last year.

Of course this guide is not just for people who were just sent home recently. It is also for people who have experienced remote work and want to become better at it. Anyone who sees themselves in a remote role one day can benefit from this guide. I do admit that some of the ideas from the previous section will repeat themselves. but it's worth reading those tips from a different point of view. So let this be a guide that not only brings you great success, but the most rewarding and joyful career you will ever have.

The management section is not just for managers

For a while I was considering making this section its own separate book, instead of bundling it after the management part. But I realized that if you want to succeed in your remote job and become irreplaceable, a key advantage would be to understand your manager. That's especially true when it comes to old-school bosses who are forced to go remote; nothing brings them more relief than to see that their employees understand how the remote world works. The reality is, if your boss does not know how to use these tools, it's your opportunity to be the superstar who introduces him to them, and can do the same with the rest of the team.

Your manager or boss might be brilliant at motivating and inspiring his team, but he might not be familiar with technology and barely know how to turn on a webcam. In the Remote Management section, we discussed how to replicate the experience of the office. Show your boss that working remotely does not have to change much of his daily routine, and outside the project management software that might require some real thinking or at least real consultation, most technologies like Zoom and Slack are easy to use. If you are in this situation, just read the management section, then you can start shining within the company. Not only is your job not going to be in jeopardy, but you might just get a great promotion and a raise.

II – WORKING ENVIRONMENT

Distraction-Free

I know you are probably thinking, what kind of technology will I be using? How will I communicate with my team and boss? How will I collaborate? Can I stay sane without hanging out with my colleagues?

These are all important concerns. But your first area of focus when switching to remote work should be to avoid distractions. Distractions most certainly are not an issue that is only associated with remote employees, it's an issue with work in general. As I explained before, in an office environment over an eight-hour work shift, the average employee produces two hours and fifty-free minutes of work, because they are being distracted by colleagues and meetings[8].

---

8   https://news.gallup.com/businessjournal/23146/too-many-interruptions-work.aspx

The stats show that it takes an average of 23 minutes and 15 seconds to get back to work after distractions.

Yet in our homes, especially these days, we are most certainly not immune to distraction. For me one of the biggest blessings of remote work is getting to hang out with the kids. For my business, that is the biggest curse. Besides doing evening work, I have to work out time with my wife to have chunks of non-distracted work. Whether or not you have these family-related goals to tend to, you still need to have a quiet, focused working environment. You can't have your husband keep on asking you where his pants are. Think about this way: If you can create a three-hour chunk of non-distracted work time in your house, you will be more productive than the average office worker is for an entire day. For all the bosses who are spying on this section, I'm not saying that it's ok to just work three hours a day. I'm saying that in temporary rough times, shorter, focused chunks of work can be the most productive way to do it.

So close yourself off, put your noise-cancelling headphones on, and if you live with other people, make sure you set the right boundaries. You can always tell your partner or kids that you will come down to hang out with them when the project you're working on is done. If hanging with the kids for part of the day is your new reality, but you don't have to be immersed completely in the kids' activities, you can use this time to make phone calls to lower-priority individuals. Considering that I'm paying their bills, this is the perfect time for me to chat with suppliers and kid-friendly colleagues.

TAKEAWAY:

In a crazy world where you can't always have eight hours of distraction-free time, try to book focused time in as big a chunk as you can. Three hours of non-stop work is still way better than five hours of stop-and-go.

Creating a Separation

For years you were taught that when you are home, that's non-working time. When you put on professional clothes, get into your car and drive to the office, that's the time when you produce. That's work time.

But now, everything has changed. We get to work from home. We get to sit on our sofa and our bed and do some work. Right? You probably expected me to say wrong, but it's not necessarily wrong. If it works for you, go ahead. But there is a small, teeny, tiny chance that you are delusional about whether it actually works. It has to work for you on two levels: productivity and mental health.

About 20 years ago, before using my phone as an alarm clock, I used a standard cheap alarm clock that made that biiiiiiippp biiiiiippp sound. I don't know about you, but I can't imagine anything that I disliked more than that machine when it woke me up. You're having the best party of your life, drinking a $1000 bottle of scotch and suddenly this annoying noise starts coming out of nowhere and steals you from your wonderful dream.

It got to the point where I would go to real parties and I could hear that awful alarm sound, biiippp biiiiipp biiiippp for a few seconds in my head, making me feel like I was being woken up again. After realizing how much stress the situation was having on me, I upgraded to a better radio alarm with music, and life was a bit easier and happier. It had become a classical conditioning situation, where I would associate that sound with negative emotions, then let those negative emotions filter into the more positive elements of my life too.

Working from home could lead to the same negative association if you're not mindful of your mental health and wellbeing. If you love your job, awesome. But for many people, the job is how you pay the bills. Not being able to separate your work from the non-working world can lead to you not being able to separate yourself from negative feelings. That could be your boss's voice ringing in your ears during a random 9:30 pm Zoom call while you're watching

Stranger Things, which is pretty much your own 2020 equivalent of that biiiippp sound.

So if you are working from home, you must figure out how to separate your work life from your home life. Unless you absolutely love your job or you're some kind of Zen master, that probably means you should avoid working in bed, and consider not working on the sofa too. Instead, establish a consistent work space and work routine, ideally at a proper desk with a proper chair in a quiet room. Some people try to do some of the repetitive work while watching TV. I question if you can get much real work done while doing that. But more importantly, there is something to be said for completely unplugging. You must create an area in your house that's for work only, so that when you're *not* in that area, you can truly relax.

When you wake up in the morning, take a shower, brush your teeth, and put work clothes on. Yes, wear work clothes. When it comes to techies who like questionable casual wear, feel free to dress like yourself — but that means gamer hats and t-shirts you grabbed from tech conferences, not pajamas or boxer shorts. Who knows, maybe you can even improve things by putting on a clean shirt, one that actually has buttons. Let's put it this way, if you find yourself getting excited by fresh underwear day, that's not good.

For all the lawyers who are forced to work from home and still need to come on Zoom every once in a while, remote does not mean casual Friday everyday day, sorry. Until COVID-19 came along to scare the pants out of us, when I searched for a lawyer remotely it was because I wanted someone cheap. If you still want to charge $300 an hour, you need to put a blazer on and behave like nothing has changed.

When it comes to the working space I understand that not everyone has the means to have a full office...but at least create a little work space for yourself. Get yourself a great desk, put headphones or earplugs on to block out sound, and if possible, get amazing headphones. If you have kids that you must listen to, then get bone conduction headphones like Aftershokz. (I use the Aeroplex and they are very comfortable.) Make this space as cool as you can, way cooler than what you have in the office. If you can, get yourself two big screens, a fast computer, and great speakers. Put up a background you like, get pictures and tchotchkes that you like for your desk — bonus points if these are items that were frowned upon when you worked in an office. This is your opportunity to have the dream working space; hopefully your company will foot some of the bill.

TAKEAWAY:

Dress like you would dress in the office.

Even if it's two steps away from the bed, create a work-only station. It is important to have some kind of separation in your life, rather than always being in action mode.

III – A Remote Worker Perspective

Communication

Just to be clear, you are not the only one who has anxiety about this entire remote thing. Actually the person who is even more concerned about all of this is your manager or boss. For many of them the concept of people working from home means a lack of control, which they hate. They feel like all the processes and culture that they have created are now in jeopardy. Some managers question if their employees will take advantage and slack off because they are not able to make sure that those employees sit on their asses and work.

Unfortunately, not everyone pays attention to how unproductive people can be in a physical office; just because someone's sitting in an office for eight hours or more doesn't mean they're putting in more than that average of two hours and fifty-three minutes of work per day. Still, for traditional managers seeing people in the office eliminates a lot of anxiety. If your boss is one of those people, the best remedy for the problem is open communication.

If your boss usually communicates with you on a daily basis, give her a Zoom link, and show her how to get the most out of Slack. By doing this you can tell her that you still want to keep up with your daily chats. When you do start up those daily chats from your home office, remember to do so on a webcam, since that tends to get the message across better than simple phone calls. If your boss likes to visit people in their office or cubicle at random times, keep your Zoom available and let her visit any time that way instead, in the form of a watch party.

I can already hear all the critics on this one. Having watch parties in the office means bringing bad office strategies to a remote environment, they would argue. But sometimes you need to show people that things have not changed much. Let people get comfortable before you start showing them what needs to be changed. Don't worry, you will not feel like you are in a Big Brother episode, because no one can spy on you. If you provide a Zoom link you get to see exactly when someone comes in to chat. Also, if your boss usually has an open-door policy in the office, suggest that she have a watch party herself. Your first goal in this case is to eliminate any anxiety for your remote-phobic boss.

One of the healthiest habits of communication is not to wait for the boss to ask for progress reports. Instead volunteer all your accomplishments, all the tasks you are working on, and let her know if you have finished your assigned tasks at the end of the day. If you do that, you are getting work done on your own terms and your boss will become less likely to bother you, much less micromanage you.

If you work for a remote-savvy company, communication becomes a survival tool. Stick to the same policy of bragging about your work, and for crying out loud whatever you do, don't disappear. If great communication is the way to make your boss feel confident, disappearing and not being accessible is the way to drive that same boss crazy. When I message my employees, I'd much rather get a message that they are busy than no message at all. We try to work in a non-distracting environment, where unless you are in the customer service and admin department, I don't want to distract you in the middle of a job. That's why active communication, which does not require the manager to bother you, is the best sort to use in remote work environments.

Keep in mind, your bosses may bring a lot of bad habits from the office experience. If you show them alternative strategies that work, they will eventually back off and start enabling a distraction-free environment.

Digital nomads can work from anywhere, but when it comes to a team meeting, you do need to maintain a certain level of professionalism. Noisy coffee shops or crowded co-working spaces might not be the best locations to dial into a conference call.

Have mercy on your colleagues and managers and call from a quiet place.

TAKEAWAY:

For extra remote-phobic bosses, try to replicate the office experience as much as possible. That includes even the bad habits, because with time, they will notice that those habits are ineffective.

Be proactive. Show what you've accomplished, rather than waiting for someone to ask you for a rundown of what you've done.

IV - Mental Health

I'm a true believer in remote work. I believe that the world will be a better place for it — a drastic improvement for the environment, work production, and family life. But there is one major negative side effect to the remote world: People are becoming less social, less present, more secluded, and lonelier. The one true positive aspect of going to the office is that it forces you to interact with people. Don't get me wrong, this forced interaction could be a big reason why you are producing less work, because of all the distractions it creates. Still, it's also one of the most reliable ways for adults to make friends and establish bonds with other people.

Like becoming obsessed with multiplayer online video games and social media, working at home, especially in sectors like programming and writing that don't require tons of interaction, can cause you to disappear into an unhealthy place. I'm not just referring to the reality that you can skip showers and stay in the same clothes for days. Unless there is a proactive measure, no one is there to track if you are eating lunch, working late, or falling into depression. It is even more challenging during a crisis like a pandemic, considering that for months we were supposed to lock ourselves at home, and even after that reduce in-person interaction.

That's why it's important for us to find new ways to socialize. Start hanging out with your colleagues and friends on Zoom, even if it's just to have a remote drink or lunch. Start a peer group for all your remote colleagues and make sure that it is an open space to discuss mental health. If you live in the same city, creating physical hangout time makes time so much more valuable, and people appreciate it more.

It's also extremely important to find some time to work out; sitting at a desk for eight hours a day practically demands that you work up a sweat, whether that's regular gym sessions or games of full-contact, underwater Scrabble. There's tons of research about the importance of preserving mental health for remote workers. Share that research with your boss, make it clear that it's a priority for you, and that in the long run it will even help the company's bottom line.

Working remotely will help you realize that you can't depend exclusively on your work for social experiences. Joining a coworking space, meeting new people on Meetup, and joining as many group activities as possible are all great ways to improve and maintain your mental health. Keep in mind that it might be somewhat harder to find social experience when you're working remotely. But at least now you have more time to socialize and take care of your mental health, considering that you are more productive and waste less travel time. While mental health is a scary aspect of remote work, being able to be in control of your social experience will lead to a happier existence in the long run. In fact, based on MIT Sloan research, remote people are significantly happier.

TAKEAWAY:

Mental health is a serious concern in remote work. Pay attention and take proactive measures to preserve that health.

If needed, try to work in a social environment. Set up meetups and hangouts.

V - APPLYING FOR A REMOTE JOB (AND WHAT NOT TO DO)

This coronavirus hasn't just sent people home. Unfortunately for many of us, it's sent some people packing. If that's happened to you, look at it as an opportunity to look for a better job, one that appreciates remote workers. As a recruiter I go through many outrageous cover letters, from people just posing questions about what would happen if they were hired without describing their skills, to people who tell me their entire love story with remote work.

While I was going to offer advice on how to succeed in an interview, I have realized that different companies and different interviewers might be looking for completely different things. Instead I decided to focus on what makes me want to rip your CV into a trillion pieces. Unfortunately most of us have forgotten the satisfactory feeling of ripping pages or hanging up the phone, so I'm simply left with criticizing. Enjoy.

Don't act like a service provider

As a boss, I want an employee, not a service provider.

One time, I interviewed this lady for a marketing position who had been juggling several projects with other clients. I asked her: "Why are you looking for a job?" She answered that she was looking for stability, which is a great answer, so my follow-up was: "What are you going to do with your current clients?" Her answer was that I would be her top priority. That was not such a great answer, and she failed the interview.

There is no question that many companies want an entrepreneurial mind that thinks outside the box, but no one wants someone who acts unfocused and independent from the company. If this lady would have answered that she'll focus only on my company, but asked if it would be OK to keep one project on the side as a low, low priority, I would have hired her. But her choice of the words *"top priority"* sounded like I would be her top client, not that this would be her actual job.

This showed me that the lady was not serious about fully integrating into our company.

No one wants a free-spirit freelancer or digital nomad

A few months back I received a letter from an applicant who told me that she would love to work remotely because it will give her the opportunity to travel and be flexible. This, ladies and gentlemen, is what I call the freelance mentality. The dream is to travel or work on the beach, to have all the flexibility in the world. It shows incredible passion for all of the things that the employer doesn't give a flying fig about.

Employers don't want someone who travels often and works from beaches. They want someone who sits on their ass and does good work. That doesn't mean that you can't take advantage and travel every once in a while. Some of my top guns in the company like to travel and even change location every once in a while. But that's a side effect that comes after you have proven yourself.

Treat the interview like an in-person interview

It continuously blows my mind with certain candidates. You don't have to drive in traffic, you don't have trouble finding the place, you simply need to turn on your computer and put on a headset. Yet so many people still find a way to get this wrong. People have this unusual habit of trying to come exactly on time, only to find that something is buggy with their computer or the conference tool, which of course makes them late.

The problem is that many people still have a "freelance outsourcing industry non-committal" mentality, where showing up exactly on time to discuss a project might seem to be a more reasonable course of action. But in a physical interview you would always show up 15 minutes early, you would dress appropriately, and try to be as prepared as possible. So why would it be OK to do anything different for a remote interview?

In a recent interview I had someone calling me from a phone where the background wind was distracting. I asked him why he was talking to me while walking around. His answer was that he went to a restaurant and didn't want to distract other people. I would have given him another chance if he would have told me that he was stuck in traffic and couldn't reach his computer on time. But not for this lame excuse.

Again, I don't want people to lie to me. But I would much rather they lie as a way of showing that they care, instead of being honest about not giving a shit.

Did I mention that when he video-called me, this guy also had three buttons open on his shirt like he was on his way to the club? Come on, man! This is your career we're talking about. All interviewers want from you is to sound and look like you care about the interview, and hopefully the job that comes after that.

Test your equipment in advance

As an extension of treating your interview seriously, set yourself up in the most tech-forward environment you've got. If you didn't get a chance to read about the Whatchamacallit Effect in the management section, read it. It's important. Realize that there are many irritants in a digital conversation that your interviewers can't put their finger on, but most of it goes back to sound quality. If they provide you with a conference tool, test it beforehand and make sure to show up 15 minutes early to deal with any potential glitches. It just blows my mind that even with techies, about one in three interviews get delayed because they don't seem to be able to get their system working. So plan ahead.

Remember these two important points: If the interviewer can't understand you, even if it's because of the technology, your communication sucks. If you make it to a digital interview late, even if it's because of technology, you are late.

Discuss what you can do for the company

All the examples and stories that I've just provided can be summarized by one phrase: The applicant did not pay attention to what matters to his potential employers.

Spend a lot of time discussing what you can do for the company. Remember in sales, it's all about you (the company you are applying for) and not about I. To sell a product (in this case yourself), you need to pitch your potential client (in this case your potential employer) on how the product can benefit the company. When you apply for an interview, discuss how much value you can bring to the client. How much you can produce, how much you can save for them, and how much you will contribute to the process and culture.

Ask questions and learn about the company

If you want to truly win in an interview, prepare questions. Not just any questions, but questions that show that you understand and are interested in both the company and the industry in which it operates. The power of asking a question instead of making a statement is that you can sound smart without actually knowing what you are talking about, and for that matter not shoot yourself in the foot when you make a potentially wrong assumption.

Asking insight questions requires both preparation and an understanding of what the company is actually doing. Make sure to visit the company's website, read the blog, and learn something special about the company that shows that you actually put in some effort. That's how you blow interviewers out of the water. As the boss of a company I have to tell you, I'm not immune to someone pampering my ego. If you've watched my videos or read my book and you tell me about it, you'll get tons of super chocolatey brownie points. Here's one small anecdote: In an interview recently where a candidate was asked if he had any final questions, the candidate asked what type of music the employer liked, knowing full well that they both like Led Zeppelin. This blew the client out of the water and certified a culture fit. Keep that in mind next you are coming to an interview.

Really, what I'm saying is that the employer on the other side just wants to feel that you are treating it like a real job. Applying for a job from home means that you need to be even more professional than you would in a physical interview, not less. If you ever come to a remote interview acting unprofessionally and you still got the job, don't feel like a winner. There is a big chance that the client hired out of desperation. Which means you are probably getting paid less than what you could have if you presented yourself better, and you might become the first one to go when there is trouble.

TAKEAWAY:

Come to a meeting 15 minutes in advance, prepare all the technology, and treat the interview as if it's happening in person. Remote employers expect more, not less.

No one wants a noncommittal employee. Don't act like an independent service provider.

VI - HOW TO SURVIVIE AND THRIVE IN A REMOTE JOB

The advice below is worthwhile for any employee, but unfortunately for remote workers, you are expected to do more. If you want to have a stable job with growth opportunities in any kind of company, pay attention to the advice below.

Learn your company standards

About a year ago, my client decided to fire a programmer on the spot who was with him for about six months. This was quite a shocker because this programmer seemed to be doing great. Every time we asked for feedback from the managers, they said he was incredibly productive, and they were extremely happy with him, so we couldn't understand what had happened.

Apparently the programmer was working on a VPN that tracked the work, and the boss decided to go on the tracking system one day and found out that the candidate was only signed in for an average of 6.5 hours per day. The programmer has worked in a more flexible environment before, where if he finished his tasks early, he could leave. Only this time, the boss really didn't appreciate it and saw it as dishonesty.

As much as I don't recommend tracking software, I can't blame this boss. What the hell was the programmer thinking, leaving when he wanted to? He should have asked his managers what their expectations were when the job is done. Of course, it would have been nice for the employer to define his expectations more clearly or at least give the programmer another shot, but unfortunately you do not always have those kinds of luxuries.

Accountability

Honestly guys, no one likes a person who always has an excuse, especially if everyone knows that you messed up. I can't say that every company has a mistake-friendly environment. But if you already made the mistake, own up to it and show how you are going to fix it. Most bosses will truly respect you for that. As a manager, always take responsibility for your team's mistakes, and reward them when they do right. If your boss does not understand the value of that mentality, it will be difficult for him to manage remotely anyway.

Analyze your failures

It's not enough to be accountable for your mistakes; you need to do something about them.

I hope you work in a company that treats mistakes as learning experiences. But whether you do or not, you *will* eventually make mistakes. How you handle those mistakes is what truly defines you. If you note down where you went wrong and show what you learned, how to repair the issue, and how to avoid it in the future, you can and will turn your mistakes into opportunities to impress.

Create backup plans

One of the main ways to show that you learned from a mistake is by providing backup plans. Losing momentum can be very costly in certain companies. For example, at DistantJob, when we need to hire someone quickly, it's always a good idea to find a backup candidate if the first one doesn't work out. Always have a backup plan in mind whenever you make a major decision.

Contribute to company culture

I'm not saying, "be the last person to get drunk at company parties". But if you are the person who always uplifts people and gets the team to connect, it will be very hard to fire you, even if you have nothing else to offer (and I'm hoping you in fact do have more to offer!). Especially in a remote world, if you introduce social activities, bring people onto Zoom for birthdays, and help foster teamwork, you become a tremendous asset for your company.

Don't be distracting

Contributing to company culture does not mean messaging people randomly at any time. Continuous pop-ups on a chat program can be incredibly distracting. Try to schedule discussions with people so you don't interrupt them in the middle of a task. Ask your colleagues what the best ways are to reach them without causing a distraction. You can also suggest they turn their Zoom or Slack to *busy* or *away* so they don't get calls or messages when they don't want them.

Text responsibly

This is definitely one of the dumbest things I do. I don't always pay attention to what I type and I don't always define the context. When you message someone on Slack, WhatsApp, Skype, or even text, just go ahead and get to the point. Type the actual subject you want to discuss, and try to be coherent. I was told by many people that it is extremely annoying to read a text that sounds like I was drunk when I wrote it; in reality I was just not paying close enough attention. Or was I?

Contribute

If you are shy, get over yourself. When a boss invites you to a meeting, more often than not he is not looking for a monologue.

Contributing to a discussion is the perfect way *not* to disappear in the noise of the remote world. Of course your contribution needs to be of value, so don't be one of those annoying schmucks who talk just for the sake of talking. Even if your contribution isn't anything special on a given day, it's still worth it to contribute, because the more your boss hears your voice and name, the more she will think of you when the time comes. Other ways to contribute are by focusing on improving systems, and bringing new ideas to the table, whether by email or through the company's internal communication system.

Share your tasks

A company should have a project management tool or some kind of system to communicate your tasks. If your company doesn't use that kind of tool, proactive communication becomes a must. Your boss will be hugely impressed if you communicate your daily tasks at the beginning of the workday; it would be even better if you also tell her what you have accomplished by the end of the day. That kind of communication can be a huge relief for any anxious boss. It's also important to share your tasks and projects with your teammates, so there won't be any redundancies.

Don't send tasks to the task graveyard

I understand we are all busy and we can't take on every task all at the same time. Some jobs seem so low-priority that they just disappear. But that task you consider low-priority might not be viewed the same way by your manager or boss. Communicate with your boss about it, and ask him if it's still relevant. Let him know on a weekly basis all the tasks that you have not forgotten, so that even if it's a low-priority one, he will know that eventually it will be done.

Take feedback well

It's tough to work with people who get sensitive or offended every time you offer any criticism or input. Don't be one of these annoying people. Yes, some bosses are just assholes. But most of us are trying to invest in making you better. Take any feedback that you get as a learning experience and ask questions. If one day your boss sees that you implement his strategies the way he intended, it will reflect well on you.

Share your schedule

Let people know your schedule. Sharing it will make you a better teammate and employee, allowing others to figure out the best times to contact you and collaborate with you. Sharing your schedule serves as both an invitation for others to reach out when the time is right, and a healthy boundary for others to respect when you're not on the clock.

Provide measurable results for your work

I wish that in real life, people used the progress bar that you often see in video games. They are never precise, but for some reason always make me feel better.

Your manager is supposed to track your progress on tasks, but that's clearly not always the reality. Being an awesome remote employee is all about doing what your manager *should* expect even if he doesn't request it. Provide a way for people to see your progress on projects that you do. Define KPIs for what you are trying to achieve, and show how far you're gone.

Introduce new tools

Remote work is all about using technology to create a professional and intimate working environment. And we are just in the beginning stage. Eventually we will have quality telepresence robots, virtual reality, holograms and more. We will have a system that tracks all our work and directs us to the right path. Recently, Facebook introduced a fully interactive camera called Portal; what a perfect way for your boss to walk around the room and chat.

Yet not all technologies have to be so serious and important for productivity. One of the most impressive technologies I was introduced to lately was the virtual version of Cards Against Humanity. With it, we can assemble on Zoom, play cards, and crack up. What could be better? If Cards Against Humanity is too risqué for your company culture, you can always find other ways to use technology for team-building purposes, in addition to boosting productivity.

Update your management system

You know a salesperson always looks like a professional when she fills up her CRM (customer relationship management software) with great updates. A remote salesman has to do better. When a company provides you with software to update your work and tasks, be more diligent. Doing so not only makes you look good — it gets you off the hook when things don't work out very well.

Ask and learn about your employer's expectations

Alright, I will come clean here. All the attributes just mentioned are the ones that would impress me and would make you a superstar in my company. But not all companies are the same. In many companies, especially big ones full of bureaucracy, there are shitty managers who just don't get it. Some will be annoyed with your positive efforts, and some will be intimidated. I find that most companies that are open to remote work have better managers and want to create happier, more independent employees. Unfortunately, that is not always the case; to discuss every company's policies and preferences would take 500 million more books.

That said, here's a great way to meet the expectations of just about any boss: be a strong communicator with a solid sense of intuition. You can do this in two ways.

First, during the onboarding process, ask lots of questions: "Do you want me to prepare a task list each morning?" "Do you want me to contribute to the company's culture?" "How do people like to interact and connect?"

Find out what the most important values are. If they say accountability and an asshole-free environment, they're inviting you to take more responsibility, and be willing to speak your mind openly and honestly.

The other way is to push really hard from day one, then get a feel for the feedback. If you provide measurable results every day to your employer and she becomes irritated anyway, she probably does not see this as an effective use of your time. You can even be transparent when you take aggressive action, asking your boss if she's happy with what you've done. Again intuition is important. Sometimes yes does not mean yes, if it sounds more like *whatever*!!!!

Get to know both your company's vibe and the manager's vibe. And always use common sense. I don't see why anyone's boss would not love it if you show proactive and independent action, but unfortunately bureaucracy does often result in some terrible managers climbing the ranks. This is my disclaimer, so you can longer hold me responsible.

VII – PRODUCTIVITY AND PROCRASTINATION

Those are the types of chapters that every president dreads. That throughout the years while you claimed to work your ass off nonstop to build a company, you were really not as productive as people would think. You know the famous stories that go like: "when I started the company I walked in the snow, barefoot, uphill both ways, to meet our next client. My office technology consisted of a rotary phone and a waffle iron."

You want people to get inspired, so you shine your reputation to make it as compelling as possible; you certainly don't want to seem like a procrastinating bum.

I grew up in a world where the president or CEO of a company needed to be the first one to wake up in the morning and the last one to leave. This was how you were supposed to inspire people, and for a long time

I did just that. I woke up around 7 every morning, no matter what I did the night before. I immediately started working, finishing my morning obligatory jobs like emails, troubleshooting with my team, and checking on recruits. I would then take a shower and then go to an office. As much as I believed in remote experience, I was quite happy having an office to go to. I always tried to have it close by, but even if it was a bit far, the journey there offered a great time to listen to audiobooks and learn.

I would start doing research for marketing strategy, then see a recommendation for a video about the topic, and watch that too. The problem was that YouTube would then pop up with a great video about cat acrobatics, then suddenly I'm watching Muhammed Ali's best fights, then a few old SNL skits, and next thing you know, the entire day is gone.

Even worse was when I tried to get active on social media for the business. That initiative pretty much lasted 10 minutes until I moved on to see what my cousin has been doing, then flipped through my friends' vacation photos, then started arguing with someone who thinks Pit bulls should be exterminated (poor dogs). But all this was nothing compared to when I decided to turn on a cute flash game. I wouldn't expect that it would eat up my time. Boy, was I wrong.

I never thought of myself as having an addictive personality. Besides alcohol, I didn't do any drugs, and I didn't particularly have bad habits, (I promise I did not inhale). But I most certainly experienced real addiction. For recurring periods of a few weeks in my life, I experienced the inability to disconnect. I would come to the office, hide my screen carefully and start playing games, stupid flash games, nothing fancy. I remember having internal discussions with myself saying, *I need to get off this and do some work* and my other brain would say, *who are you kidding, you can't get off now.* It got so bad that when I really tried hard to disconnect, I would hyperventilate and even start getting teary. It was crazy.

It's hard for me to admit, but between YouTube, useless social media debates, and video games, I have wasted entire months. When I spent an entire day playing the most addictive of those flash games, I hit the bottom. I had finished an entire day accomplishing nothing, exhausted, depressed, and realizing that things needed to change.

I began breaking down my patterns. I noticed that if I managed to avoid playing video games for a week, the addiction would go away. I also noticed that when I didn't work or even *fake work* but instead took actual time off, I wouldn't procrastinate, so I wouldn't feel the need to play the games. With that in mind, I took a few days off work, then started researching the causes and cures for procrastination. Yes, the irony was that I was procrastinating by doing research about procrastination, but it was still the best thing I could do at the time.

This research wasn't easy, because the books and blogs that covered procrastination, learning disabilities, and ADHD were often full of average advice by people who probably don't procrastinate as much. Some of them just told you that you needed to keep to your tasks and give yourself breaks to reward yourself. All of this was just a bunch of advice that almost insulted your intelligence, treating you like some kind of undisciplined idiot. Other books and blogs covered the fear of succeeding. While it's true that many people do distract themselves with a mental block that can hold them back, that's not really procrastination, and it wasn't what was happening with me.

It took about a year and a half to find the right book that truly changed the game for me. Actually it was an audiobook, which meant it only took three hours of easy listening. The book is called *Get Things Done* by David Allen. The quick summary of the book is that our brains can simply be overwhelmed with data, which can lead to procrastination.

Even a small challenge like booking a restaurant has surprisingly many steps to it and can create many bottlenecks. You need to figure out who is coming, you need to check with them. You need to check what kind of food everyone wants to eat, are they allergic to anything, are they halal or kosher then get the restaurant's phone number, and then actually call. With a burst of energy you can finish the process in 10 minutes. But when you're low-energy and your brain is exhausted, any one of these bottlenecks can create an exhausting task for your brain. I know it's crazy but your brain always wants to go to a comfortable place, and even small tasks can build up and overwhelm your brain, prompting it to run away to somewhere easier.

So how do you solve that? Make sure to keep your brain empty and note down all your tasks. Then when you are in a high-energy state, take all of these projects and break them down to the smallest micro-tasks. Checking off these micro-tasks one by one will be easier for your brain to handle.

In the past, you might have used little note memos to keep track of these micro-tasks. You can also modernize this strategy, by using phone memos on your phone and an app to break down all of the tasks. I still haven't found the perfect task app, but the closest one I've seen was Nirvana HQ. It doesn't do subtasks, but otherwise it does everything that needs to be done digitally, and yes it also has a speech recognition voice memo widget that you can put on your phone's home page.

Still, the writing down tasks strategy only works partially, if you don't make sure to empty your brain frequently and break down tasks when you're in a high-energy state. Problems arise when that high-energy state never seems to come; I quickly learned that the biggest reason for my procrastination was feeling tired. I realized that being ultra-strict about my wakeup time, even if I was up late the night before, made no sense. So for a while I started to avoid using my alarm clock. I just woke up when I needed to wake up, and holy cow, the amount of production after a good night's sleep was incredible. And the cool thing about remote is that you really can get away with sleeping more.

Still, some people do feel genuine hesitation and fear about their work. When I mentor people in business, we discuss how starting a business is so tough, that you absolutely cannot afford any excuse to hold you back. Some people feel guilty about making money or succeeding. If that's the case, you might as well give away your business idea to someone else, because it's not going to work.

While working remotely can give you added flexibility and take away some of the stresses that come with commuting, you still can't have any room for hesitation. If you fear succeeding, if you have any mental blocks at all, talk to someone and deal with those blocks, because that's what will hold you down as a moderate worker, instead of enabling you to become an amazing worker.

Another lesson I learned is that certain things you can't fight. It's funny, 15 years ago if someone accused me of having no willpower, I would either bow down in shame or try to lie to myself that yes I absolutely do have lots of willpower. Now that I know myself better, I can comfortably say that with certain things I do have little to no willpower. I don't need to try to fix myself; sometimes it's just OK to just cut certain things out of your workday, and out of your life. If you can't control your eating intake, sometimes the best solution is to keep your fridge empty. If you are addicted to some kind of drug, don't hang with people who like to get high. These don't have to be some life-ruining, mind-numbing activities either. Anything that we obsess over to the point of harm that doesn't benefit our life are addictions, and we should try to deal with them. For me, it was a stupid online game. So I just simply made sure that no game would ever sit on my computer or phone from that point on.

My director of marketing who also happens to be an expert in gaming, actually explained to me that it is the small games on our phone that are built like drugs to form an addiction, and these are the ones to avoid. So I made sure to cut those out.

But what about videos and social media? These are actually tools that I need to use for my work, both at DistantJob and for my non-profit organization. Sometimes we simply can't cut out the friends who influence us to do drugs, and sometimes alcoholics have to work in establishments that serve alcohol. I don't have a perfect answer for them, but at least in the digital world you can use apps that block certain sites temporarily, or permanently. MacOS has a great app called SelfControl.

Because I'm a Windows and Android kind of guy, I like to use RescueTime. These apps block sites that are a distraction for a certain amount of time. Again the magic of working from your own personal working environment is that you don't need to have the awkward explanation of what you have been doing before you put the block on those sites. "|Oh yes absolutely, I'm such a focused lad that I preemptively decided to put an app on my phone that prevents me from using sites that I should not be using. Yes, hmmm, cough cough."

Yes you can cheat these apps or hack these apps if you try really hard. But the truth is that all the procrastination tools that we are using affect our overwhelmed brains. If we can simply delay our brain just a bit with blocker apps, the non-addictive part of your brain can take over again. It really works.

I have to say that these days at 41, I need to use these tools less and less. My brain is better trained to be productive and just by emptying my mind from tasks and giving it energy with proper sleep and when necessary some kind of caffeinated drink, I procrastinate a lot less.

The reality is that people procrastinate heavily, and very few people are actually honest about it. As someone with an aggressive case of ADHD, I have been intimidated by people who seem to kick ass 12 hours a day. But very quickly I learned that working 12 hours a day does not mean producing 12 hours a day. With years of self-analysis and research in this department I gained confidence that most people are just not the production horses that they claim to be.

While there are some exceptional people in this world who can accomplish great feats of production, others use tricks that we are not aware of. For example, world-famous CEO Jack Welch was known to have his meetings booked all day. His job was to consult, help, and troubleshoot. I don't think he did this to avoid procrastination. But having a booked schedule sure does help, and it's a common tactic that many great CEOs use.

Looking back to my story, the work that I was doing in the mornings just after waking up was mostly operational. I was always very productive at that time, because the tasks on my plate needed to be accomplished and were clearly defined.

Knowing who I needed to talk to and what I needed to do — this kept me in an amazing state of focus. Once the daily operational tasks were done and I needed to start doing the heavier lifting to find solutions for future growth, that was when the procrastination started to happen. While I was always very good in sales (especially during conferences), I could see the effects there too: During high-energy times I would talk to anyone (even strangers), but during low-energy times I would just sit back and watch.

When my business grew and I started having a booth or having my meetings set up for me, I could work all day non-stop. I would simply have an adrenaline rush that got me excited to talk to anyone who would come by. So based on your personality, having your schedule filled with activities that make you feel productive is another amazing way to get a full day moving forward.

The reason why I'm telling you all this is hopefully obvious. You have just been forced to move home, so you have fewer people looking over your shoulder. You no longer need to put up an Excel sheet screensaver to hide your games of solitaire. (Man I'm so old, I can't believe that Excel and solitaire are the first things that popped to mind.) Now you're at home sitting by yourself and your boss is so overwhelmed, it might take him months until he figures out who's not being productive.

You can get away with so much in a remote environment. But you can also choose to take advantage of the situation and thrive at your job. You are finally in a working environment with no distractions. You can make your own routine, get in shape, create a hobby, and still kick ass at your job. Your boss might take a while to notice if you don't produce, but he most certainly will notice if your production exponentially improves while other people struggle. Switching to remote work can either be a time to get down, slack off, and become an expert procrastinator, or it could be your ticket to the big leagues. Go ahead, explore, get things done, use the tools that I suggested (or research other amazing tools out there), and try not to be another member of the two hours and fifty-three minutes club. This is your time, so go get it.

TAKEAWAYS:

If you get addicted to a procrastination tool, try to go cold turkey for a week, then regroup and strategize how to avoid it.

Based on "Getting Things Done" by David Allen: empty your mind while noting everything down and break down tasks to the simplest micro-tasks.

Get good sleep, and you are guaranteed to produce more, even working fewer hours.

Cut out distracting apps, or use app blockers if you must.

You need to do better

So many of you might be sitting and reading this book thinking, *"Wait a minute, why do I have to do all this?*

It's not my fault that I was sent home, I didn't ask for this. I'm perfectly happy doing what I'm doing right now."

Well then you need to ask yourself this question: Do you enjoy working from home? If you don't and you like the social life back in your office, then go ahead and do the same thing. I truly do believe that office work should still exist for people who thrive in an office environment. But for the rest of you, in order to survive and thrive in a remote world. you must do better. If you don't understand why, we need to go a bit deeper into boss psychology, at least for the majority of bosses out there.

If you've ever heard the phrase "out of sight, out of mind," this is what I think about when I don't want my little kid to have more dessert. But in the business world, this is a reality for many remote employees. During the COVID-19 pandemic, I have interviewed several bosses who only let some of their employees work from home, and most of them felt incredibly disconnected. So unfortunately, it is up to the employee to keep on reminding their bosses that they exist. As I mentioned earlier, taking on leadership roles and introducing better remote management strategies are how you can get there.

Another annoying insight into the strange and frustrating brains of many bosses is that when they let you work from home, they may feel like they're making some kind of grand sacrifice. Most bosses enjoy seeing people who work under them. With remote they lose a bit more control. That means they need to work a bit harder and faster. They need to *change* things that they know already work. Even with all the benefits that come from remote work, many bosses still prefer the old-school way that they've gotten to know and love.

Even some bosses who have fully embraced the remote model may feel that they've made a noble sacrifice on your behalf. They know that they've given you the best perk by allowing you to work remotely. Unlike any other benefit, including medical, insurance, paid vacation, free food, free coffee, and free Nerf guns, remote employment can't really be bought with money.

That's why most bosses out there expect something in return for this incredible benefit: great work and increased productivity. The silver lining in all of this that now you have the opportunity to create a better version of yourself. Everyone enjoys being successful in what they do, and the remote experience forces you to be just that. If you choose to work harder and become more productive, it should be because you want to gain the satisfaction that comes from doing a job well.

Your higher level of productivity making you irreplaceable in your boss's eyes is a nice fringe benefit.

TAKEAWAY:

To have a successful remote career you must do better, because inexperienced remote bosses tend to forget about you, while an experienced remote boss might feel that allowing remote work is a grand gesture.

Part III - A Few Extra Tips For Everyone Going Remote

I - A Few Big Ideas

Remote does not always mean working from home

Hey guys, I have a secret to tell you: When it's not COVID time, I work in an office. I know, I know. The guy who is preaching that working from home is the best thing since sliced bread does not actually work from home. What's up with that? Well, the truth is that working remotely does not necessarily mean working from home. That's why I choose to stick to the word remote, only a few times mentioning telecommuting or explicitly working from home.

Remote simply means working outside the office, ideally in the most productive working environment that you can find. I work one block from my office in a kick-ass coworking space. I have my door closed when I need quiet and open when I want a little more hustle and bustle. Also I have the luxury to come home for lunch with the kids. It is truly the most optimal working experience for me. So no, remote work does not necessarily mean working from home. It means working in the most productive environment you can find. I personally like my man cave outside my house, and wouldn't trade it for anything.

TAKEAWAY:

Remote means working from your most optimal place.

How does an extrovert handle working remotely?

I heard a fun quote recently about working during COVID: *"While introverts have reluctantly managed to work and even thrived in an office environment for more than a century, why can't extroverts survive the next few months at home?"*

Some of my closest friends (who to be fair are the epitome of nerdhood) feel that Santa Claus has shown up early (or a bit late, seeing as the pandemic hit in March) and given them the greatest present. This has truly become the time of introverts.

Now the big question: How did a dude with Attention Deficit Hyperactivity Disorder, who also loves to socialize, end up starting a recruitment company that is strictly dedicated to remote work?!

Honestly, I don't know myself. I don't know what I was thinking. My best guess is that it came from my love of traveling and working with people all over the world. That experience made me realize that we are truly missing some key components for a better work environment.

I would say that seeing companies with supposedly amazing culture uprooting people and their families from their community to join them at company headquarters just because they couldn't tolerate the concept of remote made me a bit angry. That anger gave me a lot more motivation to introduce a healthy alternative.

Yet the more productive question is not *why*, but *how* does an extrovert such as myself handle working by himself?

Well, first of all: *I don't feel like I'm working by myself.* I have an entire team of amazing colleagues, many of whom I consider to be personal friends. But even if you are just starting and really no one is around, there should be a plan.

Step one: If it's within your means, get yourself an office in a coworking space, preferably one that has a social environment and activities. Try to find it in a part of town where there are some bars, restaurants, coffee shops, and a gym with group activities. Yes, I'm saying group activities and not just a gym, because a gym during the day is often as dead as a concert hall during the time of coronavirus (*too soon?*). Unless you are one of those dudes who can simply make friends just by sitting at a bar, part of a successful social dynamic is working in a place where you can actually make some friends.

Also when it comes to your home, if it's within your means, live in the city. One of the interesting phenomena that I noticed growing up in the suburbs is that going out was an entire production. When you live in the city, going out for an hour to have a drink and chit chat is no longer a huge deal. When I was a single guy living in the city, I could pull off long hours without much stress...simply because my home was in the city.

As an extrovert in a remote world, there is very little division between work and life. You must book outings and activities as if they're business meetings and you must force yourself to do fun stuff as much as you force yourself to work.

Keep in mind that for an extrovert, work-life balance does not always mean working in the daytime and not working in the evening. If you can have a longer lunch hang-out and put in some extra work hours later, that too can greatly benefit your sanity and productivity. I know this from experience. Social activities such as group sports, outings for drinks, coffee, and other meetups not only lift our spirits...they also make us more productive. Sitting in the office all day without this proper balance might look good on paper, but all work and no play not only make Jack a dull boy... it can also make Jack less productive.

So in reality, you need to go out and find activities where you get to meet more people. It's good for your soul and good for your business.

TAKEAWAY:

Work and live in a dynamic environment, where going out is not a rare event.

Book your entertainment the same way that you book your business meetings, as real investments in your sanity and productivity.

Stepping into the shoes of a remote introvert

Hey there! I'm Luís, Director of Marketing and Chief Introvert Officer at Sharon's business. I'm taking over this part of the book because this fool doesn't know how good he has it.

Is Sharon seriously going on and on about finding strategies to "cope" with not having to hang out with people?! I've been trying to avoid hanging out with people for my whole life!

Here's a concept for you to ponder: You can have a life outside of work. I know, I know. It's shocking. But bear with me for a bit. It gets better. I'm going to drop a serious truth bomb. Are you ready? Here goes: *There's no rule that says that your friendships need to come from work.*

Look, if you end up meeting your best friend or a group of people that you love to hang out with at work, fine. I've made a few friends at DistantJob. The point is that I didn't feel the need to do so. I can find friends in other areas of my life, and so can you.

If you're a real professional, you are going to do your work at a high level based on your intrinsic sense of motivation. You don't need to feel that you have "a special bond" with the people you work with. All you need is to have pride in your craft! That's really it. If you need external stimuli to find the motivation to do your job, then what you need is a different job.

But motivation is just one piece of the puzzle in delivering great work. The other pieces are energy and focus. Sharon dealt with focus in the book, so I'll leave that to him and write a few words on energy.

As an introvert, other people drain my energy. That's not a judgment on people. People I love drain my energy just as much as people I hate; they just drain it for different reasons. So more time spent with people means greater energy expenditure. That's less energy available for me to pump into work.

My best days are the days where everything is solved through Slack, in the soft embrace of asynchronous communication. I can get so much done on those days, I feel superhuman! The worst days are Zoom Call Days. Seriously, a blight on the person who invented the video conference call! A 90-minute Zoom call is enough to wipe me out for the day. On those days, I have to remind myself that it could be much worse. How much worse? I could have a non-remote job.

No matter how much I complain about Zoom calls, I am still working from my home office, which is amazing. I can go out, take a walk by the seaside, and come back refreshed, ready to sit down and resume some deep, focused work. That's great for productivity, and it also makes me love my work much more!

So yes, maybe Sharon needs to find some coping mechanisms to deal with isolation. Boo-hoo. The rest of us will be doing our best work.

———————

Alright, this is Sharon. I'm back, did you miss me? Aren't you glad you don't have to be stuck with the introvert?

Joking aside, working remotely has opened my eyes to what introverts can do when you take them away from the toxicity of extroverts.

Sorry, that was a bit harsh, I'm not trying to create a new form of discrimination, we already have enough. But one of the most magical things about working with remote people is that you get to see introverts flourish. The office environment has been built for the extrovert. If you are outspoken, you will get noticed by your bosses. If you have a better ability to make friends, you will have more allies. Office politics have been incredibly toxic for companies, but there are no greater victims than the introverts, who shy away from interaction and just want to do their work. It takes a unique manager or boss to see great talents within people who interview poorly and don't participate as much in activities.

If the office is the lair of the extrovert, the home office is where introverts can truly shine. Research shows that introverts can be more productive members of the team if given a fair chance[9]. They can work longer hours on focus-driven projects, they listen better, and they think about ideas thoroughly. Because they gain energy from being alone, they almost get a superpower when you just let them sit and do focused work without intrusion. While my natural instinct in the company is to build strong team dynamics (which is why I put so much emphasis on culture), some people just need to be left alone to get some serious work done.

In the 2012 book *Quiet* by Susan Cain, the author discusses the introvert phenomenon, comparing extroverts to dandelions, in that they can thrive anywhere. By contrast, Cain compares introverts to orchids, in that both need the right environment to flourish, and both can close up if placed in the wrong environment. The office environment has given priority to the most outspoken people, people who have the charm to promote themselves. My buddy Luis is also a trained dental surgeon; yes, how crazy is it that my director of marketing can also fix my teeth if needed. But he harbors such talent in content creation and logical thinking that if I would have to function in a physical office environment, I might not have noticed him. As a manager, you should be paying attention to subtle hints of what kind of workers you have, and give

9   https://hbswk.hbs.edu/item/introverts-the-best-leaders-for-proactive-employees

them the opportunity to thrive. Remote work is about figuring out the optimal way for you and your team to work. Don't miss the opportunity to get the most out of the situation, and the most out of your most introverted employees.

TAKEAWAY:

Start noticing your introverts and see what they can do, they might just surprise you.

Introverts have an almost-superpower when left alone to do their thing; they can be extremely productive.

Brainstorming Like A Champ

I know some people love their conference room and whiteboard, but honestly, a remote working environment offers an amazing opportunity to brainstorm ideas...as long as you actually care about your team's opinions. Once you start doing *collaborative* brainstorming, you might never go back to your whiteboard.

How does collaborative brainstorming work? If each member of your staff can have two screens at their disposal (one for Zoom or another conference tool, and the other is for the collaborative app), that's a big help. The ability to see and interact with the people on one screen while contributing your ideas on the other screen is ideal. If it is beyond your company's budget, you can share your screen through Zoom or use a split-screen app to get a similar experience. I know some people also love their ultra-wide screen which could also be ideal.

Now, the first collaborative tool that probably comes to mind is Google Docs. Yes, it's an awesome program, but you don't have to stop there. There are amazing mind-mapping tools such as MindMeister and Kanban boards project management software like Trello.

When you can open the floor for everyone to insert content into a master document, you force people to think more and interact more —that's what makes the remote collaboration model so exciting.

When I want to produce some kind of document but get stuck before I could even start, I just end delegating the effort to someone else, just to get it started. I might make lots of corrections and rewrites later, but that's OK. The fact that ideas are moving forward on the page enables me to build on that momentum.

Experts in writing always say that if you want to write a book and you have writer's block, you just need to start writing to get a flow, and you will eventually get into it. This honestly works for any kind of project, and it can be a big help when someone else gets that momentum rolling for you.

A great way to conduct a brainstorming session is to pick a facilitator. Some people love to talk...this includes me. Sometimes I simply like to give long speeches; I plead guilty as the friendly neighborhood blabbermouth, and someone really should shut me up. Rather than pick someone loud like me, choose someone who is not a big talker to take on that role. That will force even the shyest person to get out of their shell. Speaking of shy people, you have to pay attention to the people who don't contribute, because you have two choices: motivate them to talk, or eventually kick them out because you are wasting their time, and yours.

If you implement these strategies and avoid useless meetings that consume your creative energy, you will never go back to the whiteboard again.

TAKEAWAY:

When you do brainstorming where
everyone can insert their own input,
it creates a much more dynamic,
collaborative experience that increases the
motivation of everyone on the meeting.
It also moves ideas along much better. All
it takes is using a webcam program and
collaborative tool.

II - Managing your kids in this new world

Ok, so at time of this writing, it's the summer of 2020. I started this book on lockdown and I promised that before I was done writing it, I would have some advice for dealing with your kids, especially young kids.

I have some great, great news: You are not doomed.

YAYYYYYY! Can you believe that?

Now that we are home, we get a chance to spend so much more time with them. The schools are giving us materials to study. Meanwhile, everyone makes us feel guilty on Facebook with all the crafts that they are doing with their kids and the lessons that they are working on. Every teacher, entertainer, and yoga instructor is inviting us to bring the kids to Zoom. But here's the reality: We need to work, and so do our partners.

This situation is made even more challenging by the risk of contagion during the pandemic, since it's preventing our parents or hired caregivers from coming to our homes to lend a hand. I feel like I'm in a Twilight Zone episode, where all the caregivers and parents are gone.

We can spare some time for our kids, but unfortunately it is not always a luxury that we have. Of course we feel guilty sticking them in front of a screen or a video game all day, where they simply become zombies. I don't know about you guys, but if you would see my oldest, she is completely a zombie, she doesn't blink. Oh man, if only there was a way to make the screen a constructive part of their day.

Your wish is my command! Turns out there are some amazing games out there that can help your kids expand their minds. With a bit of search I found incredible apps that are dedicated to teaching my kid such skills as reading comprehension, writing, and math. This includes apps such as Khan Academy Kids, Lingokids, ABCmouse, and Sesame Street. With these tools, your kids can actually learn some reading, writing, and math skills.

There are also great programs to learn different languages like Duolingo Kids and Rosetta Stone Kids. Yes, even the famous language teaching apps have kids' versions, and they're great.

Although I'm not proud of it, for a few hours a day I sit my daughter in front of those apps. Later that day, she comes back to me understanding letters in both upper- and lower-case, and talks to me about adding and even dividing numbers. She is three years old, actually writing, counting, and doing math in these games. Just this second I'm hearing her reading out loud in French. Yes, I'm bragging a bit.

That said, I have noticed an interesting phenomenon. In some of those apps there are places where the kids can actually waste time, acting like they are working. In ABCmouse there is an entire section to dress up your avatar. When I don't pay attention, somehow my girl often seems to end up on that page and hang out for hours in there.

I guess you can't do it completely hands-off, but if one of the parents checks every 20 minutes or so, you can make sure she still has semi-constructive lessons. Another piece of advice, one I got from my speech pathologist wife, is that it's much more effective for parents to be involved in the teaching, whenever possible. Show the connection and guide them through the apps. I have to say these apps make me feel just a bit less like a crappy parent. I think it's time for me to go on Facebook and make other parents feel guilty.

TAKEAWAY:

If you need your kids to do something productive, use their love of screens to your advantage. There's a huge number of educational games that real teach your kids, great skills.

II - A FEW MORE FUN TIPS FOR REMOTE WORKERS

Go for walks!

I learned this technique in one of our podcasts with Nassim Kammah from Mailchimp. I know that many people like to brainstorm around a table, but sometimes people enjoy just going for a walk and for a casual chat that sometimes brings a lot of ideas. There is simply so much research showing that walking helps come up with more ideas.

It pumps more blood to our brain, creates more connections between brain cells, and creates a rhythm for better thinking. It also manages our attention, considering that walks take only a small portion of our attention, enough to keep your mind from wandering somewhere else while you think and talk.

Walking and brainstorming is just amazing. Unfortunately, it is not possible between two remote people. Or is it?

One thing that I love to do, specifically with my Director of Marketing who's based in Portugal, is connect each other by cell phone, connect our Bluetooth headset and go for a walk in our own region. It really works and it's just amazing. These days, considering all the effort to stay at home, I enjoy washing the dishes and sweeping while talking to my VP.

Sync with your partner

During this new COVID-19 reality, how many times do both partners in a relationship have this absolutely important meeting where they can't be distracted, despite there being two kids to watch? For me, it happens every other day.

Most of us are familiar with how to use Google Calendar or any other calendar app, but unfortunately you can't share your entire business calendar with your partner. It's not because you are afraid to tell her about your secret poker game with boys disguised as a networking event *cough, cough* but because you can't drown her calendar with all the meetings you have every day.

Here's what we did at home during the pandemic: we have a shared business calendar where we put our most important *"can't be distracted"* meetings. As long as I remember to put it in there, it works and works really well. As usual, setting aside a few hours of undistracted time and booking all your meetings during this time is also a great way to be effective when both partners are busy working.

Getting in shape...remote-style!

A true remote employee master does need to leave the house, ever. They can order in, make friends, and date online.

I kid, I kid! I really hope that no one is trying to be a *"true remote employee master."* Still, in recent months it has felt like we are kind of stuck in that world, and we do need to find remote solutions for pretty much everything. One of our biggest needs is to keep healthy and sane. We can do that by working out and taking care of our health.

Yes, for the majority of us slackers, just working out by ourselves is absolutely not motivating, and just following a bunch of crazy video workouts like P90X would hardly get me off the sofa. The good news is there is an amazing solution for the nerds out there who need this extra push, especially when we are confined to our homes. It's called "Ring Fit Adventure", and it works with the Nintendo Switch. It is a role-playing game with an absolutely cheesy yet amusing story where the hero wins his battles by working out. Yeah, you heard that right. Instead of a remote control you hold this Yoga ring and have another device strapped on your leg, and you are forced to run and do squats, leg raises, etc. You even get to shoot while squeezing the ring.

Honestly I have never seen a more fun workout, and I highly recommend it to keep yourself in shape during this difficult time. If you just want to keep active, consider a standup desk with an attached walking treadmill; you can burn 250 calories per hour while working. For all of you who love to dance, there is also the famous Dance Dance Revolution, which is a really fun workout. You can also find a bunch of interesting workout games on the Oculus Quest. I'm looking forward to having a real, functional boxing or fighting game. Game companies, get on it.

Learning an instrument...remote-style!

Another quick piece of nerd advice. If you don't have kids and are stuck at home, this is a perfect time to pick an instrument. Just as I have a great game suggestion for workouts, I also have a great game suggestion for learning the guitar.

If you are one of those people who's played hundreds of hours of Guitar Hero and Rock Band and wondered what would happen if you would use all these hours to actually play a real instrument, well, here's your chance. Ubisoft has created a game for both PC and Xbox called "Rocksmith". You plug in your guitar and you play Guitar Hero-style games, but you do so by playing the real notes. Honestly, almost anything that you do goes so much smoother with a video game.

CONCLUSION

In the early stages of the lockdown caused by the pandemic, I discovered this amusing meme called "Corona Rules":

1. *Basically, you can't leave the house for any reason, but if you have to, then you can.*

2. *Masks are useless, but maybe you have to wear one, it can save you, it is useless, but maybe it is mandatory as well.*

3. *Stores are closed, except those that are open.*

4. *You should not go to hospitals unless you have to go there. Same applies to doctors, you should only go there in case of emergency, provided you are not too sick.*

5. *This virus is deadly but still not too scary, except that sometimes it actually leads to a global disaster.*

6. *Gloves won't help, but they can still help.*

7. *Everyone needs to stay* HOME, *but it's important to* GO OUT.

8. *There is no shortage of groceries in the supermarket, but there are many things missing when you go there in the evening, but not in the morning. Sometimes.*

The point is that while our elected officials behaved like everything is clear, nothing was really clear. In contrast to those mixed messages, I want to make sure that the lessons I deliver in this book are both helpful and clear.

Still, as with any topic that has lots of angles to it, there might appear to be some contradictions when it comes to remote work. I try very hard to make a point that it is easy to go remote, that it does not have to be a huge transition to a completely different way of working, that all you have to do is implement a few key pieces of technology and you can have the same experience as you would have in an office.

But then I spend pages and pages discussing things to change or improve in a remote working environment and how there are a lot of things not worth replicating from the office. I explain how both managers and remote employees have to add an extra layer of communication to their work, which kind of contradicts the concept that you don't have to change much for remote. So I feel it is worth a bit of clarification.

When you are moving to a remote environment, your first goal should be to create normalcy. Creating normalcy is about taking what you know and applying those lessons to remote. That means whatever good habits you had in your office environment, you can probably replicate most of them fairly easily with some affordable, quality technology. As a boss, even expenses should be manageable, because you will be saving money on electricity and other costs common to keeping your employees in that box we like to call the office.

If you succeed in creating that normalcy, then you are already 70% of the way to success, which is good.

Unfortunately, there is a really strange phenomenon that happens when companies start working offshore, remote, and for that matter also with contractors and freelancers. Owners and managers can spend several years and millions of dollars creating their processes and culture. These are the strategies and procedures that define their companies, and they're a big part of why those companies succeed in the first place. These leadership teams created brilliant ways to interview, motivate, teach, and operate. But when they leave the four walls of their office, for some reason they drop everything that they've learned and treat the people working remotely like suppliers or service providers, instead of key members of their team.

That's why if you just implement what you already know — including the many good habits and probably even some of the bad habits — and convert that way of doing things into a remote experience, you should already be doing very well.

I repeat: It's not so hard to succeed in making your company remote. Just ask yourself if you are getting the same positive experiences that you get in an office. If not, analyze why and plug the holes until it does feel similar, and your expectations are met within the same standards.

What makes it hard is the fear of change. People are just not comfortable with change, and whether it's rational or not, this fear is a huge distraction. When you implement change in a company, you start a new era. Unfortunately, during this *Time of Fear*, many bosses become unpredictable and become disoriented. That's why in the remote workers section I spend so much time discussing how important it is to over-deliver, especially if your goal is to keep on working as a remote employee.

If you create normalcy (which should be easy) and are able to manage the fear (which is a bit more challenging), you are 80% of the way to full remote success, and that means you truly good enough, few steps from great.

So if you don't need to make such big changes for remote, why write an entire book? The answer is to take you through that last 20%. Because from there on, there is one big change in remote work that you must pay attention to, and that is the mental state of your employees.

I'm talking about the loneliness, the separation between work and life. The potential loss of routine, which deserves more attention. Now combine all of that with all the stress and negativity arising from the pandemic situation, the inability to socialize and decompress in fun outdoor activities, and finally where applicable, add the challenge of managing kids at home, and there you go: a mental health time-bomb waiting to explode.

Mental health is a concern that should always be dealt with, especially in remote environments. But these days, if it's not one of your top priorities, then you are hurting your company.

The biggest pivot bosses need to make in this brave new world is to invest their time and train the managers to focus on their employees' personal and social dimensions. It means getting to know them better, learning their kids' names and their favorite hobbies, always asking what they did over the weekend. I'd go so far as to say you should spend the majority of your meetings learning about your employees as people. Like a therapist who discusses pleasant daily life events to find our hidden pains, you can home in on emotional challenges through the cracks. This is *the* big change, and if you master it then you will bring your remote awesomeness level up to 90% on our new remote-awesomeness-o-meter.

So how can you achieve that final 10%? You do so by using this opportunity to take advantage of the benefits of remote work. During this time when everyone is going through all these changes, there will often be fewer clients, and some belts will need tightening. That means you'll have to implement some changes to improve the situation. When you do so remotely, you'll notice that there are fewer bureaucratic obstacles.

This is the opportunity to insert some new distraction management strategies and management processes, while making sure you build and maintain an asshole-free environment. As long as many companies are laying people off, this is the time to remove the people who are making the company culture toxic, who are unwilling to change.

So with the exception of the burden on your employees' mental health, there is no need for huge change in the way you do things. Still, companies that do the best job of evolving with the times always end up on top. So take this challenging period in our lives as an opportunity to evolve.

Part of the mission of this book is to try to bring you back to the happy place where, while many things in this world are in a state of flux and uncertainty, working remotely does not have to be a source of worry. Right now, a lot of experts tell you that you should *not* try to replicate the office remotely. That you should completely restructure your way of conducting business and managing people - *because remote is a completely different world, baby!*

I'm calling them on their bullshit. Those experts might be well-intentioned, but it's still bullshit. They are trying to make you leap before you can walk, because they live in Remote Lalaland.

You can do really well by just maintaining what you were already doing, adding some webcams and chat software, and adjusting the way you deal with your employees on an interpersonal level. So there is really nothing to fear, as long as you don't start going backward. It's not that the current way of doing things is perfectly adaptable to remote work. But it is good enough. We are in baby steps mode, and to some extent crisis management mode. You can focus on transitioning to more remote-optimal processes later.

What the pandemic has given us is the opportunity to make your company something so much better than it already is, with new processes that can maximize the potential of remote work. When the pandemic is behind us, the changes that you've implemented now can pay off for years to come, with your company having become more efficient and more empathetic.

With that, I wish you the best of luck in this strange new world where remote reigns supreme. May you be happier, more independent, and best of all, much more productive.

SPECIAL THANKS

I would like to thank the following people from the remote work community for reading the early drafts of this book and providing valuable comments and feedback. You rock!

Sabina Nawaz — CEO Nawaz Consulting

Liam Martin — Co-Founder of Time Doctor and the Running Remote conference

Craig Brown — Co-founder LAST Conference, CEE at Everest Engineering

Tom Mabey — Founder/CEO Eclipse Tech, LLC

Johanna Rothman — Founder and Management Consultant at Rothman Consulting Group, INC

Appendix: Resources

Services & Apps

DistantJob — For headhunting exceptional full-time remote talent that matches your company's core values and culture — www.distantjob.com

Basecamp — Distraction-free project management built for remote — www.basecamp.com

Trello — Virtual kanban board — www.trello.com

Slack — The standard in work chat — www.slack.com

Zoom — Top-tier video conference — www.zoom.us

Asana — Robust project management — www.asana.com

Telegram — Encrypted mobile chat — www.telegram.org

RingCentral — Internet telephony for teams — www.ringcentral.com

Safetywing — Insurance for Nomads — www.safetywing.com

Books

Secrets of the Millionaire Mind by Eker, T. Harv

The Goal by Eliyahu Goldratt

The No Asshole Rule by Robert I. Sutton

Traction by Gino Wickman

Get Things Done by David Allen

Quiet by Susan Cain

Hardware

Headsets:

Jabra Evolve 75/75e

Playtronics

Webcams:

Logitech C920 series

Logitech C930

Misc:

Kubi — Telepresence Robot

Netgear Orbi — Mesh Router

Lightning Source UK Ltd.
Milton Keynes UK
UKHW021913100221
378570UK00012B/146